W9-BYK-516

Self-Made Woman

LIVING OUT

Gay and Lesbian Autobiographies

Self-Made Woman
A Memoir

Denise Chanterelle
DuBois

The University of Wisconsin Press

The University of Wisconsin Press
1930 Monroe Street, 3rd Floor
Madison, Wisconsin 53711-2059
uwpress.wisc.edu

3 Henrietta Street, Covent Garden
London WC2E 8LU, United Kingdom
eurospanbookstore.com

Printed in the United States of America

This book may be available in a digital edition.

Library of Congress Cataloging-in-Publication Data
Names: DuBois, Denise Chanterelle, author.
Title: Self-made woman: a memoir / Denise Chanterelle DuBois.
Other titles: Living out.
Description: Madison, Wisconsin: The University of Wisconsin Press, 2017.
| Series: Living out: gay and lesbian autobiographies
Identifiers: LCCN 2017010425 | ISBN 9780299313906 (cloth: alk. paper)
Subjects: LCSH: DuBois, Denise Chanterelle. | Transgender people—
United States—Biography.
Classification: LCC HQ77.8 .D795 A3 2017 | DDC 306.76/8—dc23
LC record available at https://lccn.loc.gov/2017010425

I would like to dedicate my memoir to humanity, to all of us, because in some way, I believe we are all trans. From the day we are born, to the day we die, we remain interconnected. We really do love one another, and although at times we can lose sight of that, or deny it, or turn away, we always come back to it. This fact is the essence of human existence, which has no male/female, has no gender. Yes, I believe we are all trans. In the end it comes down to embracing the "other" that is inside each and every one of us.

Contents

Acknowledgments

$\mathcal{F}$irst and foremost, my most appreciative thanks to my editor, Corey Sabourin. It was he who took my raw story and began to polish it like a stone until it became the beautiful gem it is today. He made this book really happen. Next is my publicist, Mary Bisbee-Beek. Her dedication to my public relations needs, strict attention to detail, and willingness to always be there for me as questions arose in the publication and marketing of my story allowed me to find a comfort level in the process that I would never have found otherwise. Mary made the book go! Early on in my writing, Carey Bettencourt was there to read passages and always encouraged me to keep writing. She taught me not to doubt myself and gave me strength. My close friend Becca Gillis, PsyD, was there for me countless times when doubts crept into my mind. On those occasions when I almost did throw in the towel, she, single-handedly, pulled me back from the precipice. Becca gave me hope. Authors Doc Macomber and Bob Wright consulted with me many times during my writing, always offering cheerful advice to keep me on a steady course and not wander off topic. Doc and Bob offered direction. John Brekke, PhD, read my finished section on Kauai, where we had become accidental friends, and afterward gave me one of the biggest hugs of my life. He emphatically stated that my book would change the way people think about what it means to be transgender in America. He has been with me ever since, always there for "book talk." John gave me faith. Then there was my ninety-year-old Uncle Frank Behnke, who I spoke with almost daily about the book as things heated up and publication was becoming a reality. I depended on him as a counselor and treasured his perspective and lifetime of experience. Thank you to my close friend, civil rights attorney Lake James Perriguey. From the very beginning, he patiently read my freshly penned passages and took my weekly calls offering in return his intellect, kindness, and his warm heart. Never was there a finer person, nor a more loyal friend. Lake gave me everything.

And finally, I want to acknowledge the University of Wisconsin Press and senior executive acquisitions editor Raphael Kadushin for agreeing to publish my book. When I met with Raphael in Madison, I immediately sensed a connection. At lunch while we talked about the book, Raphael mentioned that the press had never really ever published a book like this before and that they were sort of going out on a ledge with this memoir. We were looking directly at each other when he said that, and then I knew—because, let's face it, this book really does show the human vulnerability of all of us and really does put everyone on that ledge. It was not easy for me to write this book, and Raphael knows that. I really appreciated his candor that day and knew we had built trust between us.

And so it was in the very end that Wisconsin, my home state, my motherland, and the place where it all began, finally gave me the wisdom of truth. For that I will always be grateful.

Self-Made Woman

Prologue

$\mathcal{F}$inally the big day arrived and I boarded China Air for my flight to Bangkok. It was a strange flight path, over Canada with a stop in Anchorage, on to Taipei, and then to Thailand. The stopover in Anchorage was surreal. We landed in a snowstorm; it was November and even though it was only 4 p.m., outside it was already pitch black. I had a two-hour layover, so I deplaned to walk around the terminal. I was struck by how modern the airport was, but what really caught my eye were a pair of taxidermied bears, a Kodiak and a polar bear opposite one another, both standing tall. I was awed by the immense size of these beautiful creatures, their giant claws, teeth, powerful legs, thick fur, sharp eyes, and large black noses. How efficient these animals must be in the wild, I thought, saddened to find them dead inside this airport.

It could've been the impression those bears made on me or the excitement of my pending surgery once I arrived in Bangkok that brought on an overwhelming desire to call my mother. Whatever possessed me to do this I don't know, but by the time I realized it was a mistake it was too late. She had answered the phone. I immediately felt uncomfortable—why did I call her? I started off with small talk, eventually telling her I was in Anchorage, on my way to Bangkok. We'd had a few previous phone discussions about my upcoming gender change, none of which ever went well. Maybe, my thinking went, once she understood I was actually going

3

through with sex reassignment surgery—that her son was on the cusp of fulfilling a lifelong dream to become a woman—there would be some loving support. Exactly the opposite happened. I'd played this badly and my mother pleaded with me on the phone not to go through with this and "hurt myself."

Quickly, the discussion revolved around those three words. *Don't hurt yourself.* I listened in stunned silence, angry at her for not supporting me in something that she'd had hints of my whole life and was in complete denial about. On top of feeling hurt and rejected, I felt momentarily guilty over what I'd planned all these years. I was forty-nine, recently divorced, broke financially, and a recovering addict. Two tragedies in my life, an abusive father and an addiction to crystal meth, had ironically turned out to help push me, giving me the resilience to take this step. My mother still didn't understand. The call ended with the two of us as far apart as ever, but at least she knew my plans and could no longer deny my truth.

There in the terminal I stopped again at the two bears. Nothing was going to take me away from who I really was inside. I returned to the gate and got back on that plane, free of doubt about becoming Denise DuBois, and finally leaving Dennis Dubis behind forever.

It was sweltering when I arrived in Bangkok, a heat not unlike that one Sunday afternoon decades earlier when my journey began. It was the summer of 1958 and I was four years old.

My parents, sister, and I were on our way to the lake cottage owned by my grandparents. I can remember how huge the backseat of my parents' car seemed to me at that age. I recall the big shift handle on the steering column and the musty car seats. I played with the window handle, while my mother smoked a cigarette and my father a cigar. The telephone poles seemed to fly by. I counted the wires, watching them twirl and twist as we zoomed along the empty rural highway. Each time I lost count I started over again. I was very excited that we were going out to the cottage again because it meant I could play on the little dock and look out at the lake. I loved that lake. I could see all the way across it. I liked watching the wind-capped waves, the fishing boats with people rowing and the occasional outboard motor boat that always left a wake in the water. I would try to catch the dancing dragonflies buzzing around and landing on the dock, but I never could. I breathed in the scent of the fresh lake water and watched the sunshine reflect on the water and the small waves lap on the shore. I loved too the small yard that led to the lake, with its wispy willow trees whose branches snapped like whips in the wind, where Busha, my grandmother, had many Italian plum trees growing whose fruit I loved to eat. (In fact, my earliest memory is of being under the kitchen table of our house in Milwaukee on South Thirteenth Street, eating a piece of bread with Busha's plum jam on it. I must have been three and a half. I ate the whole thing and crawled out from under the table and asked my mother and aunt for another piece. They laughed and gave me one.) In the yard at the lake cottage I was always on the lookout for the familiar shade of purple that meant the plums were starting to ripen so that Busha could make her jam for me.

Summer gatherings at the cottage meant plenty of alcohol, card games, and Polish food—cold blood soup, kapusta, pirogues, cooked beets, mock chicken legs, raw hamburger with onions— all piled on platters set on a long table. Adults drank constantly and played cards, while pretty much ignoring what the kids were up to.

On that particular Sunday, my sister and I were playing on the dock without supervision. I hadn't learned how to swim yet. As much as I liked the dock, I was afraid too. The water looked so deep, dark, and forbidding between the wooden planks. I remember sitting down on the edge, next to a small boat tied to the deck, and feeling the hot planks on the back side of my upper thighs as my tiny legs dangled over the water. My sister, only nineteen months older than me but much taller, had climbed down into the boat. She was urging me to do the same. I feared the worst. I had a premonition of falling in and drowning, but eventually she coaxed me into complying. I put my hands on the edge of the dock and tried to stretch my legs down to the boat. I was shaking; my legs were too short to make it. All I could do was get one foot on the edge of it, and when I released my grip on the dock, the boat pushed away.

I went into the lake like a bag of cement. I thought I was about to drown, to die. In fact, I was about to be reborn.

In Bangkok the next morning I met with Dr. Chettawut to go over the plan, which would start unfolding later in the day with pre-surgery prep work. I was struck by how young the doctor was and impressed by his extensive knowledge about sex reassignment surgery, or SRS. He had an engaging manner, spoke proficient English, and patiently answered all my questions. He also reviewed my paperwork, which included a letter of recommendation from a psychiatrist, who happened to be the mother of one of my roommate's back in New York. She had been thorough in developing her recommendation, asking many questions about my life and how my RLE and HRT had gone. RLE and HRT are two crucial stages for anyone seeking gender reassignment surgery. The first, which stands for real life experience, demanded that I live fully as a woman for one year. The second, hormone replacement therapy, added medications to the process.

Dr. Chettawut was satisfied. "You make a good candidate for this surgery," he said. I did have to sign the usual releases of liability, however, in case something went wrong while I was under. The entire operation was expected to take about six hours. I knew this was no simple procedure and I was entrusting myself to Dr. Chettawut's skill. I also had to pay in full at this time, and since he didn't take checks, I handed over the large sum of cash I'd brought with me. The transaction felt odd. I watched the doctor's wife count the bills, something she was quite good at, I noticed.

With time to kill before being admitted to the hospital I visited a shopping mall located next to my hotel. This was a part of the Bangkok I didn't see when I passed through the city many years earlier. The mall was enormous, sleek and sexy. The stores were like what you'd see in the United States, but even more stylish and attractive. I wandered into a salon that offered mani-pedis, had one done, and then decided to have my hair trimmed and styled. When the attractive stylist handed me a mirror to view the results, I was dismayed by how short my hair was. The last thing I wanted on the eve of a sex change was hair that looked gender neutral! I had spent two years growing my blonde hair out, and in just one hour I was back to practically square one. Pretending to like it, I sulked out, self-conscious about my appearance. Back in my hotel room, I packed and then went down to wait in the lobby for my ride to the hospital from Dr. Chettawut's wife.

During the drive I refocused on what mattered. This is it, I thought, as we rode along hectic streets, passing areas of the city I remembered from a different time, a different life. Arriving at the hospital, I was struck by how ultramodern it looked from the outside, even more so than many U.S. hospitals. We didn't bother to use the front entrance for the usual check-in processing. Dr. Chettawut had hospital privileges here, his wife explained, so we entered via a side door and I was taken directly up to my room. It was spacious and bright, with huge windows that gave a view of the skyscrapers of downtown. My bed had an inflatable, alternating pressure mattress to help prevent pressure sores during my recovery, during which I'd be on my back, knees up, for five days straight. This was absolutely necessary to allow for proper healing. The room was private—no sharing with another patient—and there was access to English books and magazines. I noticed a big screen

TV and thought how handy it would be in the coming days of bed confinement.

As Dr. Chettawut's wife prepared to leave, I asked her how the hospital staff even knew I was here, since we had yet to even see a nurse. She smiled, told me to relax, assured me that the staff knew I was here, and then she was gone. I poked around my room, checked out the bathroom, and turned on the TV. There was cable and plenty of U.S. channels. I propped up my pillows and was watching a rerun of *The Beverley Hillbillies* when in walked two of the hottest nurses I'd ever seen. Their uniforms were exactly like what I'd seen in porn magazines. I mean, they were so attractive I felt compelled to ask them if they were actual nurses, which they confirmed in broken, giggling English. Next came the best part; they were here to shave my pubic hair! I could not believe these gorgeous nurses were here to do this "chore." I eagerly spread my legs, and they lifted my hospital gown. One of them said, "Oh, cute panties." That did it. Despite the Androcur, a testosterone blocking drug I was taking, I felt my penis growing hard. I laughed. It was like a final curtain call for my last hours as male. The nurses were gentle with me, using a straight-edge blade, and laughed at my half-erect penis, cluing me in that they'd seen this all before.

More nurses visited to take my blood pressure and temperature. They chatted with me, always smiling, all beautiful and young. I couldn't help but compare them to what we had in the United States. Well, there was no comparison. Thailand was just a younger country population-wise and it showed in the staff at this hospital. Later, I couldn't sleep and mentioned it. In minutes another hottie appeared to administer a shot in my buttocks. I awoke the next morning a bit disoriented, but the beauty pageant began again and I was fine. Dr. Chettawut showed up for a final discussion before surgery. He asked me if I had changed my mind. "Nope, not at all," I replied. And with that confirmation it was all systems go. I was transferred to an operating bed and moved into the preop room for my general anesthesia prep work.

In my final moments of consciousness, having been given a relaxant via an IV and feeling loopy, I jokingly instructed the staff to make sure they used enough stuff to put me under, even as I resolved to resist falling sleep. The last thing I remember was looking up at the white ceiling in this cold, sterile room and seeing a giant green gecko just sitting there. How did that gecko get in here I wondered, and then nothing, complete darkness.

Back at the lake, I had lost my footing and I was drowning in its deep, dark depths. I remember going straight to the bottom, screaming and struggling. My eyes remained open and I saw bubbles and lake water surrounding me. I remember choking and gasping. Then suddenly I could breathe—I could breathe underwater. Out of nowhere a green tornado had begun to form and swirl around me. I blinked my eyes in amazement, as it kept moving around me. There was an air pocket between the water and myself. I remained very scared but somehow sensed that everything would be okay.

I heard people screaming up above. I wasn't paying attention to them, however, I was fascinated with this green tornado, thinking I should just go with it and forget about what the muffled distressed sounds above were all about. Then I heard my mother yelling, telling me to put my arms up. Seconds later I found myself flopped on the pier like a beached baby seal. My mother had grabbed my arms and yanked me out of the water. At least that's what I believe happened. My mother offered another, lighter, version of events in which my father jumped in to save me, but only after he removed his wallet from his trousers. But I don't recall my father on the dock.

In any case, after nearly drowning, I found myself on the dock soaking wet, spitting up water. Everyone was making a huge commotion about what had just happened. Then *it* happened. I was whisked—snuggled up in my mother's arms—toward the cottage. Anyone still drinking and playing cards would've surely stopped when I was brought through there, probably still coughing, or even crying. My mother carried me into a dim bedroom and laid me down. My wet clothes were removed and taken away and put in the dryer. Meanwhile, I couldn't just lay there naked; that would not have been right. So I was clothed in the only child's garment readily available. I was put in a girl's dress. That was the *it*—the earthquake that weakened the façade of Dennis and began my decades-long transformation into Denise.

I must've been left alone to rest. The adults would've wanted to resume their drinking and cards, the kids their own games. How I loved the way that dress felt! At some point, I got out of bed to gaze in the mirror hanging on the door and marveled in how it looked on me with its ruffled shoulders, how the breeze blew underneath it, how it swirled about as I spun myself around. I knew in that moment I was a girl and the dress would always be part of me. That summer dress felt electric and in that moment, probably for the first time, I recognized myself. This is me, I thought. This is right.

Gender roles were very strict in the Polish Catholic community I was raised in. I remember always wanting to be with the women at family gatherings like this one. Sometimes I would not be noticed and could listen to their conversation, learning about things every young girl has the opportunity to find out about from her community. But sooner or later I was always forced back to the poker table, to the men with their liquor, cigars, and cigarettes.

Nearly drowning had opened up a new world for me, but in this cultural environment it couldn't last. What happened next was predictable. Once my regular boy clothes had dried I was told to put them on. I became very upset, saying I didn't want to wear those anymore because they were boy clothes and I was girl now.

My father, plied with shots of whisky, was furious. His angry stare told me that I was not going to win this duel, and reluctantly I did as I was ordered. I knew my mother wouldn't intercede on my behalf. She was a young woman and most likely was pretty drunk too.

My father and mother displayed no tolerance toward my wanting to be a girl, either in that moment or others that followed. Their attitude didn't undo anything. My feminine side was born that day and remained alive inside me.

In my hospital bed on the morning after my surgery, I slowly moved my arm, letting my hand creep down across my stomach toward what had been the ultimate objective. A big smile spread across my face as my hand gently moved around the smooth, bandaged mound between my legs. I finally had my vagina. Tears of joy ran down my cheeks. I had never given up on my dream, from that day on Busha and Jaja's dock at the lake cottage in southern Wisconsin until the day I had my surgery in the exotic city of Bangkok. Now my quest was over and my destiny had come to pass. I wanted to jump off the bed into the air, do a somersault, and run down the hall yelling the words "I am a woman now!" I could feel my new life opening up before me. At the same time there was much in my past that would not be transformed, that would keep trying to drown me if I let it. This is the hard truth and the core of my story in the struggle to become Denise. Eventually I would find a place of beauty and inspiration where I could write down the often painful events of my life, examine behaviors that were self-destructive, delusional, even illegal. Fifty years of battles—inner and outer. That nurturing place turned out to be in Hawaii. On the island of Kauai I live in an area of coastline with treacherous currents, whose name in the Hawaiian language means *unfriendly water*. Maybe that's what drew me here; maybe I wanted to be close to dark waters that reminded me of my past, of waters that had tried to drown me many times. I was saved once by the green tornado in the lake. To survive what came later, though, I would have to rescue myself.

These pages are a record of that journey: from male to female, from Dennis to Denise, from darkness to light, and from many lies to one truth.

Part 1

1958–1972

I looked on my dad as a god. I can remember a winter blizzard in Milwaukee when I was quite little. The mounds outside the window were piling high, the sidewalk and driveway were completely buried, and both the back and front porches were completely drifted over. We couldn't even open the doors because there was so much snow, and it was bitterly cold outside. But standing at the front window, I suddenly saw my father out there with his push shovel. He was wearing his full Russian coat, the kind World War II Soviet army soldiers wore, with the big belt wrapped around his waist. The coat hung down to his army boots, and he also wore a Russian-style rabbit fur hat cocked on an angle on his head and a pair of wolf fur gloves. He pushed that shovel into the heart of the biggest snowdrift I had ever seen. The man I knew, the one who left the house every workday at daybreak to drive to the AC Spark Plug plant and punch in as a tool-and-die specialist, was transformed. My father was battling the blizzard. From my warm dry spot, I watched him attack that drift, push after push after push, thinking to myself, there is no man more powerful on earth.

We moved to the suburbs on July 1, 1959. After a twenty-minute drive, we arrived at our new home, where I would live for the next fourteen years—and my parents for the next four decades. The three-bedroom, one-bath house with a big open basement was part of a new suburban development named Greendale. The area had an older section from the 1940s, but my dad had purchased a brand-new home for $29,000. Our house was in a neighborhood that was just getting started; it was one of five completed dwellings on the street, called Oriole Lane. We had moved into a construction zone. The streets were gravel and dirt, and our front and back yards plain dirt. No trees, shrubs, nothing, just the house standing there. Inside, the floors were made of fresh pinewood, and we had a modern GE electric oven and stove, as well as a brand-new shiny GE refrigerator. I marveled at how new everything was. Still, I would miss our old place: the grand cherry trees, swing set, sandbox, the electric buses going by, sirens, people walking on the sidewalk, my bedroom, and all the nooks and crannies of the old house. Where would I sneak off to now and then and pretend to snap my fingers as I muttered, "Son of a bitch," a secret habit. On our first morning in Greendale I went out to the backyard and noticed the woods a few hundred yards from our property line. I saw a red-tailed hawk flying in circles above the trees, and immediately I began to wonder what else lurked in there.

Red-tailed hawks were familiar to me from family outings to pick wild mushrooms, another lake activity. I especially loved it when Busha and Jaja joined in. They had learned this skill growing up in Poland and were happy to pass on their knowledge. Busha was a loving person. She always smiled at me and was very outgoing, even while attempting to communicate as best she could with her broken English. She had a contagious laugh that seemed to go on forever. With twelve grandchildren to dote on, coming in and out at any given time, she reminded me of a hen with her chicks, and never more than when she laughed. How I loved to hear Busha laughing. Mushroom picking happened in late October, when the leaves had turned brilliant colors, creating a rainbow on the forest floor as we stepped along it. We brought pillowcases for carrying the mushrooms and butter knives as the weapon of choice in our hunting. I specialized in spotting these mycological morsels under the canopy of dead, brown leaves. The mushrooms blended in visually, and I had the keenest eye. Once I found a patch, it was easy to get possessive about the take, even if the day's harvest would later be divvied up. One time I was filling my pillowcase with beige-tan honey mushrooms when Jaja walked up. Apparently, I wheeled around, snarled at him, and told him to get out because this was my spot.

Eventually, my grandparents sold their lake cottage and moved back into the city; they were getting too old for country living. While I was saddened to lose the cottage, outside of the one traumatic experience I had there, I loved that place.

$\mathcal{A}$ painful fact of my childhood is that my parents repeatedly denied who their son really was and wanted to be. I exhibited other behaviors besides an interest in dresses that must have raised concern but were likewise never openly discussed. One day a couple of months after we moved, Cindy, who had been an upstairs neighbor in Milwaukee, came with her mother for a visit. Cindy and I ended up wandering around the houses under construction nearby. We were picking up nails and pieces of wood when suddenly I asked her if she wanted to see my "beep-beep," as I called it. She didn't understand what I meant, so I pulled my pants down to show her. It didn't stop there. Another urge expressed itself, one that might have been related to an incident with Cindy's mother, who had recently beat me with a fly swatter for misbehaving. I asked Cindy if she wanted to spank me. I recall a strange sensation going through me, perhaps my earliest awareness of sexuality. She stared at me for a few moments and then left. I knew I was in trouble because I was certain she'd tell on me, which she did. As soon as I got back to the house my mother took me into my room and asked what had happened. Of course I lied about everything—the start of another pattern. Playtime with Cindy was over for that day and for good. Later, my parents treated me very coldly. I felt extremely guilty over what I had done and didn't know how to fix things. Their silence and avoidance hurt. I already had no one to talk to about my yearning to be a girl. Now this scolding after asking a girl to spank me further isolated me. Loneliness was setting in.

I had to repeat kindergarten in Greendale due to its different school district rules. I loved nap time and rolling out my green and red mat on the floor to sleep on among the girls, whom I preferred playing with over boys. My parents were determined that I get a Catholic elementary school education, and so the next year I transferred to Saint Alphonsus grade school. I got excited at the idea of wearing the traditional Catholic schoolgirl uniform for first grade—white blouse, plaid skirt, and bow in hair. The girls also had a particular hat they were expected to wear to Mass, which was celebrated every day at school. Of course I didn't get to wear any of these clothes. I had to wear boy clothes. But I wanted nothing to do with boys because I wasn't one, and I avoided them as much as possible. Mrs. Mertens, my teacher, allowed us to sit wherever we wanted and I purposely chose a desk in the middle of a group of girls. That year I got As in my subjects, conduct, effort, and religion. No one at school had yet flagged me for wanting to be with the girls, so I was a happy and well-adjusted student.

Then in second grade, everything changed, making the next seven years at Saint Alphonsus horrendous. Sister Vivian must've been around seventy years old, meaning she had to have been born sometime in the 1890s. She noticed that I preferred being with girls and made it her mission to separate me from them, even forbidding conversation with them. I instantly began to rebel, thereby becoming a favorite target of hers. One of Sister Vivian's favorite punishments was to have me stand with my face against the blackboard in front of the class, then she would draw a circle on the board with the chalk and make me keep my nose in that circle. She frequently walked up to my desk and pounded her bony fingers into the side of my head, yelling that I had no sense in me, no sense at all. This nun actually turned me away from God, though not so much that I didn't pray for a gorgeous white dress to wear for my upcoming First Communion. "My God, you've finally come to me," I prayed, and I meant it.

For an occasion like First Communion, my staunchly Catholic family celebrated in a big way. A party was held at the house and relatives came from both sides of the family—a rare event, as there was much discord between them. Except for these milestone occasions, they didn't intermingle. Tables were set up on the back lawn and then loaded down with food. It was a beautiful late spring Wisconsin day; winter finally felt gone for good. I was the center of attention. Whenever the doorbell rang, I stood with either of my parents to meet and greet the new guest. Being shy, I didn't like doing this, but it was necessary if I wanted to get my First Communion cards. Since every card contained hard cash, I listened carefully for that doorbell, which produced one of those funny 1960s chimes. For many guests, this was their first look at the new house that my parents had painstakingly furnished and organized. My dad and mom enjoyed ushering arrivals through the living room with its red-and-orange-striped couches, maple coffee tables, an oversize table lamp in the picture window, a bright blue vase with a long neck (into which I frequently threw bits of trash as it was a convenient receptacle), and the old cactus we had in Milwaukee, still in its red planter on black rod iron legs. I greeted each new person or group with a smile, said hello, got my card, and then ran off to my bedroom to open it. Many of the cards had $5 or $10, but some had $20 and even $50. Astounding. I had never held so much money in my life. As the afternoon wore on, poker games started up. The men drank beer, and the women sipped grasshoppers or Tom and Jerrys, each frothy cocktails that looked innocent but were loaded with booze. The Communion cards kept piling up, and my grand total surpassed $500! I was elated. Once the party ended and everyone had left, my father told me to bring all the cards and money down from my room. He went through everything, counted all the money, and when he was satisfied, he handed me $10, keeping the rest. He took my money without saying a further word about it. He was drunk, and when he saw my crestfallen face, he got angry. As usual, my mother managed to disappear just as he started to beat me.

That beating wasn't the first. One of the most shattering events of my childhood happened soon after my near drowning. We were still living in the old house in Milwaukee. One afternoon my mother and sister were getting ready to go shopping for school clothes. I was mad that my sister was going to get new dresses, shoes, underwear, socks, the works—which I wanted too. I raised a fuss, pleading to be allowed to come along. I wanted to try on dresses and see all the frilly fun things a girl gets to handle and experience when shopping. My father was in the master bedroom watching television, but he was also listening to my noisy protest. When he entered the room and my mother said it would be fine if I came along, I knew she sensed what I did: my father was not safe to be around. At that moment he erupted. He bolted into our midst and pushed my mother and sister out the door without me.

Now it was just the two of us. Though petrified, I tried not to show it. I went to my room to hide, hoping he would resume watching TV and fall asleep. I was not so fortunate. Soon he called for me. I remember emerging from my room but hesitating at his bedroom door. He had such an evil look as he coaxed me to his bed, a place I didn't want to go. If he lunges toward me, I thought, I'll run to the door and out of the house. I was that afraid of him. He was clever and pretended to have what looked like a piece of chocolate candy in his hand. I fell for the ruse and went in. He grabbed me at once and threw me on the bed, covering me with his entire body and whispering, "I've got you now! You're not going anywhere."

Did he understand why I wanted to go clothes shopping with my mother and sister? Was that what set him off? I started screaming and pounding my tiny fists against his hairy chest, but he buried my mouth under a pillow until I couldn't scream and I was surrounded by darkness. I felt so alone, afraid and helpless. There was no one around to save me from my own father. Then— I must have fainted or passed out from lack of oxygen—there was only darkness. When I regained consciousness, he was asleep on the bed next to me. Terrified of waking him up, I very quietly slipped off the bed and sneaked out. I went back into my room and hid until my mother came home. I never said a word to her or anyone else about what happened and really can't say if my father beat me that day or not. The details, though still haunting, aren't sufficiently clear in my mind. The episode taught me one thing: never trust your own father again—or any other male. That day began a lifelong mistrust of men, attributable to the central man in my life, my father, the hero who had battled the blizzard. Our bond was broken.

In a separate occurrence around the time we were preparing to move to Greendale, my father took me along on a bank errand. The bank was located on South Twenty-Seventh Street, a good mile from our house. After he parked three blocks away, I asked him how come he never got lost driving the car around. He found my question funny. What happened next though was anything but humorous. He got out of the car and began walking quickly toward the bank; I couldn't keep up. I began crying and then started screaming for him to slow down, but he only went faster until I lost him on the sidewalk. By luck I looked up and saw the bank. Inside, however, I still couldn't find him. I went back out onto that very busy city street in absolute panic and sat down on the sidewalk bawling. An elderly woman came over, calmed me down, and ended up walking me home, no easy feat since I had misjudged the number of blocks and had to coax her along until at last we were at my back door, through which my father appeared with a look of rage. The Good Samaritan tried to reassure him that I had caused her no trouble and was a very courteous boy. He behaved kindly toward her and insisted she wait by his car so he could give her a ride home. As soon as she was out of earshot, he told my mother, "You beat him first, then I'll beat him when I get back."

My mother didn't beat me that day, showing some compassion, but my dad kept his word.

I wasn't the only recipient of his rage. He beat my sister and mother on a regular basis and was verbally abusive to all of us. His violence instilled in me a sense of worthlessness at a very early age, and despair began to build up inside. This manifested itself in strange ways. Like the "son of bitch" muttering habit. I would go to a corner of the kitchen and, making sure no one was around, I would play at snapping my fingers (I couldn't do it correctly), saying, "Son of a bitch!" I did it very theatrically, getting the right look on my face, a look that had the effect of imbuing the words with hatred. One day my mother, stealthily observing me, followed me into the kitchen just as I was snapping my fingers and uttering the phrase. She beat me and then washed my mouth out with soap. She likewise had a temper, and it showed often.

The place I felt happiest during my childhood and adolescence was the woods behind our house. It was there that I had my earliest encounters with animals in the wild, a source of enthrallment my whole life. My parents bought me a bow and arrow set—my birthday is four days after Christmas, so it could have been for either—when I was nine or ten years old. This was the real thing: a fiberglass bow with a wax string and steel-tipped arrows that were stored in a quiver, which I strapped to my back. I had never considered bow hunting before but thought it might be like fishing, which I liked, so I set out one morning like a character out of the popular TV show *Daniel Boone*, starring Fess Parker. I went further into the woods than ever before. As I was standing near a huge dying tree, I heard a loud screech and saw the biggest bird ever alight on a branch about ten feet above me. It was resplendent, with beautiful light brown, tan, and white feathers on its overcoat and reddish white ones on the belly. The tail feathers were a distinct red. Its huge yellowish clawed talons that gripped the branch told me this bird was a hunter, a ruling predator of the woods. Its curved beak was huge and sharp, its eyes a piercing, clear brown-yellow. It started to preen itself until I moved ever so slightly and then it stopped, those radar-like eyes focused on me. We held each other's gaze for several moments, me because I didn't know what to do. Suddenly it stretched its wings out and lifted itself up into the blue sky, screeching as it flew away, saying goodbye. It was a red-tailed hawk, the same bird I saw that first morning in our new house. I spent many hours of my childhood and adolescence in these woods; it was a refuge where I sought safety and privacy to be myself.

Things at home weren't always bad. Wisconsinites had a peculiar tradition back in the day, particularly those who lived near the Illinois state line, known as "oleo running." Oleo was a brand of corn-based margarine, and in our household oleo running was a family event. Between 1895 and 1967, colored corn-based margarine was illegal in the Dairy State for masquerading as butter. Despite this, it was also quite popular and significantly cheaper than the real thing. My father organized oleo runs every couple of months. We kids were props, packed into the car to look less suspicious to the imagined Wisconsin State Oleo Patrol that was on the lookout for types like my dad.

The state line lay thirty miles to the south, and as we approached it, my father would say without fail, "Help me watch for cops." After crossing into Illinois, he exited the roadway almost immediately and pulled into a dingy-looking gas station. Hopping out of the car, he'd walk over to a beat-up car where a man calmly sat waiting. The man would open the trunk, which was fully loaded with cases of oleo, usually available at two or three different price levels. My father always got the cheapest. He'd pay in cash and quickly step back to our car, where my mother sat waiting with a worried look on her face. One never knew if the oleo patrol might be watching from some distant point with binoculars, ready to radio us in.

My father put our two cases of the contraband into the trunk, covered it with several blankets, and further hid it with the spare tire. The return trip was the dangerous part, so in order to avoid the oleo patrol, and perhaps to make it a little more fun for us kids, we always stopped at the same hamburger place on the state line. We all trooped into the restaurant like nothing was amiss, each of us looking about for anything unusual or suspicious. I always ordered a cheeseburger, fries, Coke, and a chocolate malt. As we casually ate our food, my father cast frequent glances out to the parking lot. If the coast was clear we'd pay up and hit the road. Rumor had it that you were safe several minutes back into Wisconsin. We were never busted, but later in adulthood it interested me to consider how my first taste of lawbreaking happened under parental supervision.

$\mathcal{A}$ more wholesome rite of passage in Wisconsin was learning to ice skate. My initial attempt didn't go well. A neighbor gave me an old pair of hockey skates, but these have no ankle support, so you already needed to be a proficient skater to handle them. Then at Christmas one year I got my first pair of figure skates. My sister also got a pair. Mine were black and hers were lily white; you can guess which pair I liked best. Still, one touch of the blades, so tapered and sharp, and I couldn't wait to get on the ice. We had two skating areas within a short distance of the house. Whitnall Park was the preferred one because it had an island that you could skate around or cut across walking on your skates. There was a shack heated by a wood stove where you could sit on a wooden bench, put on your woolen socks, and lace up, leaving your boots in a numbered cubby hole. There was always a lot of commotion in there with people wanting to get out on the ice and others wanting to come in from of the near-zero outdoors. You could hear the clunking of skates on rubber mats, and lots of excited chatter filled the large room as skaters tried to balance upright and make a quick exit onto the ice.

I learned to watch for the Milwaukee County trucks outfitted with huge bristled ice shavers that resembled giant rolling pins. These machines repaired the cracks, dents, and small holes made by all the skate blades. A different truck came by with a cylindrical polisher that smoothed the ice until the top layer sheened like crystal. The best time for skating was after these wonder trucks did their magic. I could skate fast, do complete body turns, skate in tandem, cross over, skate backward, pretty much anything. I loved being last in the chain of skaters for crack the whip and getting pulled around by the centrifugal force created when the chain made a sharp turn. All the latest pop music blasted from a loudspeaker at Whitnall, and one snowy night I remember being mesmerized by a song called "I Want to Hold Your Hand," sung by a new band from England called The Beatles. There was another reason I liked skating so much. Out there on the ice pond I was able to play with girls unnoticed. Everyone was wrapped up like a mummy, so it was hard to recognize who was who. On the ice, I forgot about hating being a boy because I could feel like a girl.

At home, too, I never passed up a chance to be around women. My mother belonged to something called Club. It was a group of her girlfriends who had started getting together soon after high school for a monthly social and had kept it going through the years. They did a round-robin, so sometimes it would be held at our house. I loved it because my father would always disappear on those evenings and I could sit in the room with all the ladies and listen to them talk and feel as though I was one of them. But when I turned twelve, I was blocked, excluded. My mother told me I had to go downstairs to the basement or to my room and leave them alone. I was devastated by the new rule and being pushed away yet again from the feminine world that I so desperately wanted to be a part of.

The summer between second and third grade my parents signed me up for little league. I was horrible at it and felt completely out of place; it didn't help that all I had for a glove was a catcher's mitt. I played right field, where all the worst players were always stuck, and never once caught a fly ball or grounder. I wasn't any better at hitting the ball. The only time I got on base was if I got walked or hit by a pitch. Mostly, I simply struck out. The constant jeers, laughing, and name calling by my own teammates and the other boys made me feel worthless.

Meanwhile, my father had begun doing the same to me at home. I now entered a period of indentured servitude to him. There's no other way to describe the endless number of chores that filled the hours of my days. The first big project that I had to help him with was building a rec room in the basement. He had ordered a huge amount of wood, and one day he began drilling holes in the tiled cement floor and pounding in 2 × 4s with concrete nails. My job was to hold the light for him, hand him nails, get more nails when needed, hold the wood while he sawed, and get more tools. If I didn't do each task the right way, I got yelled at and called names. "Idiot," "moron," "asshole," "stupid dumb-shit." He called me just about anything that entered his mind. He would also hit me on my upper arms with his fist, leaving me with large bruises. The rec room included a drop ceiling, bar, back bar, lighting, veneer and pinewood walls. It was his obsession. I dreaded going down there with him to suffer hours of being continually berated. I could do nothing right or correctly.

He did do one nice thing. When the rec room was finally completed—it took over a year—he bought me a woodcarver's set along with some balsa wood to carve with. I was touched by this act that showed some gratitude and kindness toward me. All I ever really wanted was for him to love me, but never once did he say he did. Such a simple thing could've made all the difference.

*M*y chores multiplied. Gardening, which had started off as a pleasure, turned into agony. I was put to work in the yard not only to help plant the garden but also to maintain it, as well as all the new trees and plants my father and I had already put in. My expanded list of duties included weeding, fertilizing, watering, lawn mowing, edging, tree trimming, harvesting the fruit and the garden vegetables, planting bulbs, and putting chicken wire around the trees for the winter to keep the rabbits from eating the bark. I also had to help out painting the entire house both inside and out, cleaning the outside house windows, and cleaning the rain gutters. I became invaluable too in the garage, for my father never took our two older model cars in for service unless the repair work was beyond his knowledge. Tune-ups, oil changes, switching the cars to snow tires in the fall, washing and waxing, all done by him with me assisting by holding a light on the engine or under it, fetching him tools, trying to be an able helper and forever being put down or hit by him. He was relentless. And there was still more work: cleaning the garage every spring, changing the winter storm windows to summer ones all around the house and vice versa, digging up the all plant bulbs and storing them in the basement for the winter, shoveling snow off the sidewalks and driveway, and later, when I was older, using the snow blower (in addition to repairing electrical appliances, tuning up the lawn mowers and snow blower annually, and preparing the lawn each spring with fertilizer). My cash allowance for each week consisted of one dime for each grade level I was in, or thirty cents per week that summer when I worked on the rec room.

School was no escape. Fourth grade with Mrs. Schultz was a year of punishments. She would take a page out of one of our reading books and have me copy it as many times as there was a check for disobedience after my name on the blackboard. Many times there were ten or more checks. I was out of control and acting up every day. Some days, I was placed out in the hall with my desk, which I kind of liked because I didn't have to see Mrs. Schultz. I was also placed in the wardrobe closet, where I was forced to stand for hours, all this time missing out on valuable classroom work, interaction, and socialization with the other students. I also had to sweep the floor on my hands and knees with my bare hands during class, up and down the desk rows and around the legs and feet of my classmates. For the first time in my life I was starting to feel sexually turned on by being humiliated. I couldn't quite know what is was then, but something was happening inside of me. Like my father, it seemed this woman was totally out to break me. Another tactic she used to humiliate me was to put me over her knee in front of the class and spank me to the jeers and laughter of my peers. She made a big deal of it and was very ritualistic about it. I had that faint first stirring of sexuality in my crotch area when I was over her knee. I liked getting spanked by her. I found it arousing, even though I was still too young to do anything about it.

That year, on November 22, the school principal, Sister Henri-Anne, came on the PA system to announce the death of President John F. Kennedy. I made a grand motion of dropping my Planters

Peanut pen onto the floor and gasping; I had developed a flair for the dramatic and was always seeking attention. We were let out of school early, and when I got home I discovered my mother crying over the news. I had a picture of JFK on the wall in my bedroom and stood in front of it. I remember having this feeling that things were going to change in America really fast. We lost our innocence as a nation that day.

The following summer my mother enrolled my sister and me in day camp. She was also one of the camp chaperones and went with us each day. I wasn't sure I would like it, but what a surprise when I boarded the school bus for the forty-five-minute ride to camp and it was full of girls. I was in heaven until I had to sit next to the only other boy besides me. I wanted to interact with the girls, but they all ignored me because I was a boy. "No," I wanted to tell them, "I'm not a boy, I'm a girl." My favorite part of the bus ride was to and from the camp because we sang songs, so at least I could sing with the girls. There was one song where all the girls would turn and look at me at the words "a naughty little boy"; they giggled and laughed at me every time the phrase was sung. I felt embarrassed, but again there was that faint stirring in my crotch area that I couldn't understand, though I knew it felt good.

On the first day of camp, six or seven school buses headed out in the early summer morning. I was so excited at the idea of playing with all the girls for the next three weeks. I was imagining all the fun things we'd be doing, but then after we arrived I was suddenly segregated from the girls and sent over to an area for boys only. I hadn't figured on the other buses having boys, but they did. There were about eight of us total and we had an elderly male chaperone, retired obviously, who was going to teach us how to do "man" things, as he put it. I was devastated. Our little camp was up on a hill overlooking the girls' activities, which only made things worse for me. I could see them, but couldn't be there with them. Down below they were having fun playing games, singing, learning to sew, and dancing. Our chaperone emphasized the separation of the boys from the girls, remarking on the superiority of our spot above and up away from them. If only he knew how much I longed to be with them. By now I was beginning to hide my true feelings. I had reached the stage of feeling guilty and embarrassed about who I really was inside. The socialization process of separating and defining the genders was having its intended effect on me, and I was being pushed into the deep and dark closet, just like the one Mrs. Schultz kept me in that year. I was miserable up on that hill the entire duration of camp but never said a word to my mother about it. She didn't want to hear any more stories from me about wanting to be a girl. The only thing I enjoyed was the bus rides because at least I could be with the girls then, even if they ignored me.

Given my disinterest in boys and total ineptitude at team sports, it made sense that I was drawn to more solitary activities like fishing. We took several family vacations to Ontario, specifically to fish for northern pike and walleye. These are delicious freshwater fish that thrive in northern lakes. The Canadian area we went to was all wilderness with only a dirt road leading to the cabins. Early every morning I would get up with my parents to go fish with them in the small boat provided by the resort and outfitted with my father's little 3.5 horsepower outboard motor. As we went out onto the lake, I peered over the edge to see the wake spreading off the keel. The water to each side looked deep, dark, and mysterious to me. I felt a tinge of fear, recalling again my near drowning experience, and quickly looked away from the water.

I remember catching my very first northern pike on one of these mornings before my parents caught anything. Trembling with excitement as I felt the rod bending and the reel screaming,

I locked the reel and began hauling in that fish. Every once in awhile I had to release the reel lock and let the fish run out the line again to tire it more, then start the process over again. Finally, it was up against the boat, and I could see its dark body and its colorful scales glittering in the sunlight as my father dipped the landing net and scooped it into the boat. My eyes nearly bulged out of my head. I had never seen a fish that big in my life. It flopped around in the boat, its big eyes staring at me in confusion. I could see its sharp teeth where the red and white daredevil lure was hooked into its jaw. Suddenly, I just wanted to let it go because I felt sorry for it, but I said nothing to my father as he clunked it on the head, forever silencing it. It was a giant to me, maybe eight pounds, and I was still shaking with excitement when it was all over.

Our supper, early and always very punctual, was a family affair. Neck bones were one of my favorite family meals. I didn't realize that my mother chose this weekly staple out of necessity. Neck bones were cheap and helped stretch the food budget for a family of six. That full kettle of neck bones in boiling broth, steam swirling upward, was put at the center of the table. The bone broth was joined on our table by a gigantic bowl of mashed potatoes, bread, butter, salt and pepper, milk, and Kool-Aid. Each place setting had a deep soup bowl with a big spoon. There was also a big empty bowl to receive the discarded neck bones. The feast was on! But, first, grace: "God is great, God is good, let us thank him for our food, Amen." Short and sweet.

I always started off by filling my bowl with a mountain of mashed potatoes, pouring the neck bone soup over that, and then grabbing about three neck bones. Because they were hot, you had to start with the soup and potatoes before working your way into the neck bones. I added a ton of salt to the bones to complement the huge glass of iced, sugary Kool-Aid. The trick to eating neck bones was to break them down; as there wasn't much meat on them, you had to tear them apart to get a better angle on the bigger chunks. All around the supper table you could hear the sound of bones breaking, mouths sucking and slurping, and the occasional "Oh, I got a big piece of meat!" I had no time for such useless gibberish. No talk for me; I just kept eating. This was neck bone time, and I was a pro at getting my fingers deep into the bone and pulling it apart, or, if that didn't work, bringing in the heavy equipment—a butter knife—to break it apart. I was the champion neck bone eater too, far outpacing anyone else at the supper table in terms of volume.

Afterward, staring at the huge pile of gnarled, discarded neck bones overfilling the big bowl, I often thought that a cultural anthropologist should attend our neck bone supper some time to study and analyze how a modern day Homo sapiens family could suddenly revert to a Neanderthal one, as they sat there using their hands to gnaw on, slurp, and suck on bones, and then bask in the feeling of tribal connection and a full belly.

Second to Christmas, the Fourth of July was my favorite holiday. In a town like Greendale, our nation's birthday was celebrated with all the patriotic bells and whistles. By day the revelers attended events in town and by night there were block parties back at home. The summer I was ten, the annual neighborhood party was held in our backyard, which meant that our lawn was going to be the scene of numerous grills cooking homemade bratwurst, hot dogs, hamburgers, and sweet corn. There would be tables loaded with potato salads, pickles, Jello dishes, cakes, and pies. Naturally there was a beer stand with a keg and a bar with every liquor imaginable, as well as bottles of soda on ice for the kids.

I busied myself that day preparing the front yard. We had hundreds of little American flags to stick in the ground, plus a huge flag to hang reverently in front of the house. I completely covered the yard with flags in sets of two, three, and four. Up and down the street the neighbors likewise put their flags out, creating a red, white, and blue extravaganza. Even with a war heating up in a faraway place called Vietnam and beginning to get more airtime on all major news networks, there was no shortage of patriotism on Oriole Lane in 1964. This Fourth promised to be extra special for me. Using money earned from picking strawberries—my first paid job—I had gone to a fireworks stand and spent all of it on snakes, sparklers, smoke bombs, punks, sparkle showers, Roman candles, and whistle bombs. Fireworks were the best thing about that holiday.

Greendale's parade ended at the village hall, where free vanilla and chocolate ice cream cups were handed out. I went through that line five times—looking down or hiding my face to avoid recognition—before moving on to the game booths. I had a stash of nickels for the coin toss, whose top prize was a giant stuffed dog. To win, the nickel had to land on the center on one of only two red dots on a huge board full of dots. I casually tossed my first nickel. It hit the board, rolled along on its edge toward the center, slowed down, and fell dead center on a red dot. I couldn't believe my luck. The booth manager stopped all the other nickel throwers and cleared the board with a giant rubber squeegee, leaving my lone nickel sitting out there alone, smack in the middle of that red dot that wasn't much bigger than the coin itself. Getting on the microphone he made a huge deal of my win, saying, "Ladies and gentlemen, we have grand prize winner of one of our giant stuffed dogs." The green toy with bright white eyes and a red ribbon around its neck was nearly as tall as me. I actually had trouble carrying it home, where my father, not believing my luck, accused me of having stolen it.

I refused to let his sourness upset me and entertained myself with my fireworks. When my brother joined me, I showed him how to light a punk. This was a miniature cattail that's thin and pressed. A punk burns like an incense stick, but lasts much longer and is used to light other fireworks. Since it wasn't dark yet, we did snakes. These small black cylindrical cones produced a heavy ash that held together, creating the effect of a black snake as it burned up to a foot long. The residue left a black burn mark on the sidewalk that could take the rest of the year to wear away. Next we fooled around with Roman candles, long tubes with a fuse that would send up colorful fireballs fifty feet into the sky.

As darkness approached, our neighbors gathered and excitement built for the fireworks show mounted by the village of Greendale. Music blared on a record player my father had set up on the patio, and guests danced to the albums by bands from the fifties. Everyone was getting drunk, smoking cigarettes or cigars, laughing, talking loudly, staggering around, or too drunk to stand. My mother, an attractive woman in her prime that summer, got not a few invitations to dance from the neighborhood men emboldened by liquor. She obliged, and I was so glad to see her happy. One of the male guests kidded my father about needing to keep an eye on his wife so she didn't get stolen away from him. The remark was all it took to set him off. That snaky jealous side of him switched on. He watched my mother closely, growing angrier the happier she looked. I saw him pour yet another stiff drink and knew this didn't bode well.

A deafening kaboom in the northern sky marked the start of the big fireworks show. Folks refreshed their drinks, including my father, now with a permanent scowl. But the fireworks distracted me from his dangerous mood. They filled the heavens with their kaleidoscope of colors. I loved the loud sounds, the chorus of ooohs and ahhhs of the onlookers. My favorite fireworks were those that exploded and then broke into smaller ones with a distinctive whistle sound before breaking again into explosions of red, white, and blue. Another favorite I called the spider. The flare shot straight up, higher than the others, before exploding and filling the entire sky with gigantic orange daddy longlegs.

The finale marked the end of the long day and began a steady exodus of our guests. By this point, if my mom even spoke to another man, my dad glared angrily at her. I worried that once everyone was gone, our protection of adult eyewitnesses would be gone too. After the last revelers left I went to my room, where my prize stuffed dog awaited me on my bunk. Hoping for the best, I drifted off to sleep. Then mayhem erupted. I awoke to my mother screaming down in the living room. I lay motionless in absolute terror. I was scared for her and myself. Many times a nighttime argument begun by him would sweep up me or my sister: the bedroom door would slam open, and there would be my father yelling at me to get out of bed and come to the living room, or the "death room" as I got to calling it because of those terrible inquisitions.

His rage tonight remained squarely on my mother. In a state of intoxicated jealously, he accused her of getting close to other men while dancing and then he punched her—producing the scream that had woken me. I listened as he railed on, punching her again and slapping her. Despite her sobs, I remained in bed, feeling too vulnerable to intervene. He continued to verbally abuse her and he threw her to the floor—I heard her body thud—before kicking her several times. My father was a drunken bully who beat helpless women and children, and I wished him dead that night. Thankfully, there was sudden silence; the nightmare was over. In the morning, proving that the awful event had been real, I saw my mother wearing a scarf to help hide her bruises. She looked so defeated that I almost cried. I wished she would divorce him, so we could all move away forever.

By this point in my young life I was certain I'd never be a normal boy. I no longer just thought about wanting to wear girl clothes but did so. I would sneak into my sister's room when I was sure she wasn't around, rummage through her dresser and closet, and hold up items in front of her mirror to see how I looked. I imagined myself dressed up with makeup and long hair or a wig. My next step was to go into the bathroom, lock the door, and put on my mother's cosmetics. I got very good at sneaking around; no one in my family of six noticed a thing. This fixation on being female had begun playing out outside the house as well. At school I started entering the girls' bathroom. Initially I just wanted to hang out in there: look around at the pink walls and tiled floor and big mirrors. Gazing at my reflection I imagined myself in the girls' school uniform of plaid skirt, white blouse, ankle socks, and shoes. My fantasy self had shimmering hair and plenty of makeup. If I entered the bathroom after school hours I sometimes sat on the floor for twenty minutes or so, thinking about what my life could be like if I were only allowed to be a girl.

My mother took a part-time job at Dooromatic, a new assembly plant located in Greendale. I took advantage of her absence from the house and skipped class, or rather, escaped Sister Catherine, the latest teacher who had it in for me. She liked to walk up to my desk, grab my hand, and press down with her fingers into the center of my hand or grab a finger and pinch on it to do the same. She also would grab my upper arm and pinch my skin to inflict pain, trying to get a reaction out of me. At times it worked and my eyes teared up in front of the class. This became her preferred way of controlling me. The weird thing was, I grew to like it. I started to enjoy the pain she inflicted on me, and I was enjoying the humiliation of having it happen before my classmates. There was a strange pleasure in all of it.

It was more than just my treatment by the nuns that turned me off to the Catholic Church and religion. Once a year the Saint Alphonsus donation report arrived in the mailbox. I was old enough to recognize how disingenuous the booklet was, which masqueraded as a simple report, letting each family know how much money they had donated in the past year. In reality, it was little more than a way to shame them into donating more, given that every family's tithing was listed for all to read. We did so ourselves. As soon as the booklet appeared, we looked up our neighbors and friends to see how much they gave. I found it repugnant that this information was made public. It was another hypocrisy that soured me on Saint Alphonsus and the Catholic faith.

$\mathcal{M}$y skipping of classes escalated in junior high school, especially once it became clear to me that following morning roll call, there was no more attendance taking, even though we switched classrooms three times a day. I grabbed my sack lunch and sneaked out between classes or at recess and went across the highway that separated the school from the woods. I would fix up a spot to lie down, eat my lunch, listen to the birds, feel the wind, and watch the leaves and branches blowing about in the sunlight. I was close enough to school to hear all the kids playing, but I wanted nothing to do with them. When the weather turned colder, I sometimes went home, since my mother was at work. It felt strange to be there alone during the day. After lunch I ate some ice cream, being careful not to eat so much that it would be noticed. I was constantly on guard in case someone came around. Besides watching TV, particularly *Dialing for Dollars*, a show that came on at noon and featured cash drawings, I listened to a half-hour local radio show called *Feminine Forum*. It was an all-women show about everything from clothes shopping to menstruation. One time I called in and actually got on the air. The hosts made quite a fuss about having a man, as she stated it, on the program. I mumbled something about how women were changing things too fast in society, and they politely discussed their view on the issue. Why had I said this? My comment didn't reflect my real feelings; I saw women as the superior sex.

During these afternoons I stole into my sister's bedroom and started dressing, going the full distance for the first time. I put on her panties and bra, followed by nylon stockings. I learned to gather and firmly hold the rolls of stocking for my feet, careful not to get a run in them as I pulled them up over my legs. I would try on several of her dresses, skirts and tops, and began to get into putting on makeup. I loved experimenting and learning what worked best for me. Using eye shadow and mascara took practice, I discovered. Every minute in her room I was always very nervous for fear of discovery. Afterward, I showered and returned to school. I was usually gone about three hours, including recess. Sister Catherine knew I was cutting class and didn't seem to care. She was happy to have me gone.

The next summer we did a two-week family road trip to Yellowstone, with sightseeing stops in Iowa and South Dakota. After visiting such classic spots as Mount Rushmore, we reached Yellowstone with its fabled Old Faithful geyser. The cabin we stayed in at the park was a short walk to Yellowstone Lake. After supper I would go down there on my own and sit on the rocks, watching the golden sunshine dance on the lake and pondering my life. I had reached an age to reflect, and I had plenty to reflect on. One sore subject was Kitty, a cat my father had returned to the farm where we had got her after deciding she couldn't stay and that I subsequently rescued and brought back. Fresh sight of the kitten in our house made my father livid. He came straight at me and it was clear to me then that this was not going to be a regular beating. He bloodied my face with his fists, knocked me to the ground, pinched the roll of my stomach fat (I had been gaining weight), and yelled obscenities at me, finally hauling me up from the floor only to kick me as hard as he could in the groin so that I collapsed, lying doubled up in pain. Then he drove off with Kitty and dumped her—I never knew where. This man had such rage inside of him! This wasn't even the only such incident with a pet. He had previously killed my three baby rabbits, drowning them in the sump pump of our basement, where I later discovered their tiny floating corpses.

The harder reality I reflected on those evenings by Yellowstone Lake was the knowledge that I was different from other boys. I had deep feelings of wanting to be a girl, was already dressing like one, and it was becoming my big secret. I didn't have an answer to who I was anymore, and I was feeling more and more guilty and ashamed. Staring out over the water, I asked myself, "Where am I going to end up?" I was afraid for the future and where it might take me because I knew these feelings of wanting to be a girl were not going to go away.

We continued our vacation, following the highlighted map in the Triple A booklet. Our 1959 Ford Galaxy took us south through the Grand Teton National Park, where mountains with wizard-cap tops majestically rose from the valley floor. I wanted to pull over, lay down in a meadow, and soak in the wondrous landscape. But my parents, bent on getting home as quickly as possible, were not up for any unnecessary breaks. In eastern Iowa we stopped for the night. The last two days had been marked by arguing parents and fighting kids, so we were all glad the Best Western had an outdoor pool to help everyone cope with the muggy heat. A big surprise awaited me at that motel pool: a girl. Other than wanting to be one, I had never had any romantic feelings toward a girl until now. There was something about her that attracted me, and the whole family noticed. Immediately, I was the target of teasing. I didn't care; all I wanted was to get to know this girl. I went back to our room to change into something that hid my belly fat to appear more appealing. Back at the pool I sat in a lawn chair next to her. Nothing happened. We both just sat there pretending to be interested in what was happening in the pool when it was obvious we wanted to talk. Finally, we made small talk about our respective trips and then said maybe we'd see each other later. Throughout supper all I could think about was my crush. Afterward, with dusk falling, I went back out to the now deserted pool area. There she was sitting in the same spot, looking even more beautiful in the fading light. We held hands, talked some more, and then kissed— my first kiss. I floated back to the motel room in a fog. We left early the next morning, right after breakfast. I never saw that girl again, and don't even remember her name, but part of my childhood got left somewhere out there on the Great Plains.

As soon as I was old enough to babysit, I tried it out and liked it. I also liked the money I earned. One family I sat for regularly was comprised of a divorced woman in her early thirties and her five-year-old son, both of whom lived with the grandmother, herself widowed and playing the field just like her daughter. I was mostly needed on weekend nights, and because the two women came home late I would sleep over in the guest bedroom. Eventually I began snooping around the divorcée's and grandmother's rooms. The divorcée had some beautiful lingerie, skirts, tops, dresses, shoes—and she was about my size. The grandmother had a walk-in closet full of amazing wigs. The bathrooms were loaded down with makeup: foundation, eye pencils, eye shadows, mascara, lipstick, lip gloss, perfumes, nail polish, and more. I was in heaven.

My cross-dressing on the job started off slowly. I would put on a little makeup, a touch of perfume, and go back to watching television. The kid, I made sure, was always fast asleep. Soon the lure of these girl things became overwhelming and I got bolder. Spending more time trying on wigs and clothes and makeup also meant getting the boy to bed quicker, so I would play fewer rounds of the board games he liked. I tried different wigs and styled them with hair spray, being careful to note how they looked beforehand so I could restyle them afterward to their original appearance. I was so pleased by what I saw in the mirror: a pretty girl turning her head from side to side, smiling wide. With such a large variety of cosmetics to play with I sometimes did three makeup changes per night. In case someone should come home early, I kept makeup remover, several washcloths, a towel, and tissues handy in the extra bathroom for a fast cleanup. Another adventure was the foundation garments in the grandmother's bedroom. She had all kinds of corsets, girdles, and support bras to get that perfect feminine figure. After making my choices, I'd stroll over to the divorcée's room and have my pick of the hottest fashions of the day. I loved the miniskirts, tight tops, boots, and high heels, which I wore with her panty sets complete with garter and stockings. Accessories came next. I would hit the jewelry department in both bedrooms, decking myself out and then taking a few minutes to touch up my makeup and wig at the full-length mirror. Back downstairs I'd open a can of soda and return to the living room to watch TV. I was a girl now and sat on the comfy couch with my legs crossed, feeling so right, so on, so there, and so content. I would relax and think about how I could do this permanently. How could I cross the divide? How could I do this for good?

One night while lost in my daydreaming fully dressed I looked up from the couch and there was the kid staring at me. He stood in front of me with the most quizzical look. "Dennis, are you a girl?" The question struck me as such an innocent, natural one, without any malice or harmful intent, that I just wanted to hug him and say "Yes! I am." But I needed to lie, so I gently took him by the hand and led him back to his bedroom, telling him on the way that he was only dreaming, and now it was time to keep dreaming in bed. As soon as I'd tucked him in, I rushed to the bathroom in a panic, removed the clothes, scrubbed off the makeup, and then put everything away and went to bed myself. The next morning, a Saturday, I rose early enough to leave before anyone else was up. I left there a nervous wreck, having no idea what the boy would tell his mother.

I didn't have long to wait to find out. That afternoon I got a call from the divorcée telling me to come over, smartly using the excuse that I had forgotten the money that was left for me on the table. I rode my bike at a very slow pace, contemplating if I should even show. I rang the doorbell and the door opened. Seeing her standing there with the kid behind her bearing a worried expression on his tiny face I knew she was onto me. "Were you wearing my clothes last night?" she asked. I denied it. "Have you ever worn my clothes?" Another denial. Her son, she said, woke up last night and saw me wearing her clothes. I told her that yes, her son had woken up, come into the living room, and asked me, for whatever reason, if I was a girl. I explained that I could tell he was dreaming and helped him get back into bed. My lie didn't wash. She slammed the door in my face, accompanied by a look of disgusted contempt.

The burdens I knew I carried since that day on the dock were becoming harder to bear and harder to hide from the world.

$\mathcal{F}$reshman year at Greendale High School started off disastrously. I had gone out for junior varsity football but hated the head coach and the practices so much that I quit by the second or third week. As the fall progressed I became desperate to break out of my self-imposed exile and signed up to work on the freshman float for homecoming weekend. It was a brilliant move. The float was being assembled in a garage just up the street from my house and the crew was mostly girls. I enjoyed the job. It was very artistic, and we handled lots of green and white crepe paper, which were our school colors, scrunching it up and gluing it into the chicken wire that provided the outline of our design. A classmate I liked had also volunteered. Although she came a few nights, we hardly talked as we worked side by side. About a week out from the big school weekend, the float was done. I was really proud of it but sad there would be no more evenings with the girls.

As homecoming approached I asked my crush to go with me to the bonfire, which was a sort of pep rally. She said yes! Then I asked if she wanted to go to the game the next day and she said yes to that too. I was stunned. I didn't have the nerve to ask her to go to the freshman dance the next night mainly because I was afraid of the freshman football players who would be there. They were still gunning for me for quitting the team; they regularly harassed me in gym class, in the halls, at lunch, and after school if they could find me. The Friday night bonfire was a big deal in Greendale. The site was an empty field next to the school, and a massive amount of wood, from finished scraps to logs, comprised the pyre, atop which was placed a dummy football player made of straw that represented the opposing team our school would be playing the following day.

My date met me on the bridge over the Root River. It surprised me how beautiful she looked all dressed up. As we walked silently toward campus, I got up the nerve to take her hand. Despite how cold and sweaty mine was, she let me. At the event we participated in the tug of war battle against the sophomore class, laughing and loosening up even as we lost. I noticed ugly stares from other freshman boys when they realized I had a date. Being one of the few in that category made me feel older and more mature; I felt above these mean-spirited boys for a change. My date and I walked hand in hand to the bonfire, with the Greendale Fire Department on hand to supervise the burning. Engrossed by the spectacle of the huge flames dancing toward the top of pyre and igniting the football dummy, I didn't notice the group of boys that had gathered behind me. One by one they began to assault me discreetly by kicking the backs of my legs and kneeing me in my buttocks. My date had no idea what was going on and I did my best to act like nothing was happening. I endured the abuse until I could hardly stand up, at which point the bullies vanished.

Fearful of a new attack, I didn't want to risk walking around to look at all the floats on display, including the one my date and I had spent time on. All the fun had gone out of the evening for me. I asked myself why I was even here, since I didn't belong. I was different from everyone. I wanted to be a girl, and I liked wearing girls' clothes. Why was I putting myself through this by pretending to be someone I wasn't? My self-reflection was brutally honest that night but also hard to live out. Because, like most kids my age, I wanted to fit in and be liked. I said goodnight to my date, who continued to be unaware of anything, and managed to get away from the area without further incident. For the homecoming football game the following day, I had already purchased a pair of tickets and was supposed to meet my date at the entrance to the field. Though part of me really wanted to see her, I was too scared of being a target again. I stood her up, seeing a matinee instead. Afterward I felt horrible whenever I saw her in school. She either ignored me or gave me a dirty look. My standing in the freshman class sank even lower.

*M*y father's abusive behavior continued unchecked. One Sunday afternoon, I came home and glanced in at my parents in the living room. I noticed my mother had tears in her eyes and asked what was wrong. Instead of her answering, my father did, declaring that she was fine. I then spotted a drink on the coffee table and, most upsetting, a bruise on my mom's arm. I was barely out of earshot when he started up again, calling her names and saying she was fat. My brother was in our shared bedroom and my two sisters were hiding in their room too. I wished I had never come home, that I was anyplace else but here. Suddenly, we heard our mother scream as our father struck her again. Then all hell broke loose. Mom came running down the hall screaming at us to grab whatever clothes we could because we were "leaving for good." Dad, meanwhile, laughed sarcastically, yelling, "Leave for where? You've got no place to go."

We drove into Milwaukee, all of us with grave expressions, and parked at McDonald's. I went inside to place the family's order, bringing back food that we ate in the car in silence. It was difficult to enjoy the meal; we had none of the usual enthusiasm for the hamburger chain's cheap and tasty food. Mom then started talking about Dad in frank terms for the first time ever in our presence. It was as if she were half talking to herself, half to us. At least it was something. I was in the rear seat with my younger siblings and our older sister was up front. She lamented ever marrying our dad. She said she wanted to leave him but didn't know how; she had no way to support us, no place to go, no one to help us. It was such a sad expression of being defeated that we all started to cry with her. She told me, as the eldest son, that at least I could get out of the house by joining the army in a few years. This statement made me realize how clueless she truly was about who I was. If she only knew that she really had three daughters instead of two, I thought. Her lack of understanding was partially a testament to the façade that I had built to keep others from knowing the truth. I was, by choice, putting myself deep in the closet for fear of others discovering "my big secret." The Stonewall riots were just about to happen, but it was going to take a long time for any of that to filter back to sheltered Greendale. I was on my own in this journey, and while I had known this for some time, that day in the car eating hamburgers and crying with everyone, it hit home.

We spent hours in that parking lot: the five of us staring idly ahead, trying to figure out what to do. It grew dark, and then darker still. The moon was out when Mom finally started up the car. We knew where we were going and nobody had to utter a word. When she pulled up to the house, not a single light was on, yet we knew the beast was inside because his car was in the garage.

We all tiptoed into the house, and my mother bravely turned on the kitchen light. He could spring out from anywhere, I thought. Then we heard the television in the bedroom, a good sign; he had passed out. In the morning I could hear my parents downstairs in the kitchen. As a young child I had found comfort in overhearing them in the very early hours: Mom making coffee and Dad getting ready for work. Today it was the same, like nothing had happened. But something had, and I redoubled my resolve to leave this house as soon as possible.

I masturbated for the first time one afternoon during the summer between my sophomore and junior years. I was in the basement sitting around bored when I started playing with myself. Before I knew it, I was down on the tiled floor, on my side, stroking myself to orgasm. The second I came I knew I'd be doing this again. Indeed, masturbation quickly escalated into a compulsive behavior, and though this was perhaps not unusual for a teenage boy, in my case the activity served as a means to heighten and reinforce my feelings of wanting to be a girl, elevating daydreaming to sexual fantasy rewarded with intense bodily pleasure.

I soon had a stash of panties and bras hidden in the basement, all stolen from a friend's older sister's bedroom, from my own sister, and—in a new high risk behavior involving trespassing—from apartment basements. I pulled this off by finding an unlocked door to the basement of an apartment house, usually one near the woods, as that made a quick escape easy. Each apartment in the four-flat had its own laundry chute from the apartment to the laundry room. Tenants would throw a cloth bag full of dirty clothes down the chute, where they would stay until laundry day. Once in the basement, I unzipped the bags of dirty clothes and snatched several pairs of panties and bras. It took nerve to do this in broad daylight, and the more often I did it the more addictive it became. Masturbation sessions would follow at home in the basement with me dressed in the panties and bras, with another pair of panties placed over my face, their scent arousing me further. Soon my fantasies found me being forced into bondage, dressed, and spanked by a woman. All this compounding behavior—the stealing, the fetish fantasies, the ongoing desire to be a girl—had the effect of alienating me from regular life, which was already so fraught with problems. My self-esteem plummeted. I wasn't even seventeen yet, and suicide began to enter my thoughts.

I did try to end my life one time there in the basement. I took a piece of wire, made a hangman's noose, put it over a beam and then around my neck. I slumped down but before doing so, yanked down my pants so I would be found wearing my panties. It wasn't long before I started to fade as the wire cut off blood circulation to my brain. Everything became fuzzy. I saw white stars before my eyes. I was close to passing out when a voice started counseling me, telling me it wasn't my time yet, that I had to stand right now before it was too late. I struggled to grab the beam and loosen the wire around my neck. Slowly, I stabilized myself. I undid the wire completely and moved to the couch, where, rubbing my neck marked with a ring from the wire, I cried and rocked myself. I purged all of my clothes after this incident, tossing them in a dumpster. No more stealing intimate apparel, I scolded myself. No more masturbation. I swore off ever wanting to be a girl and told myself I'd never think that way again. I was certain that this was behind me now; I could go on with my life. But as would become my pattern, I was unable to follow through on my intention.

Another element to my cross-dressing both thrilled and frightened me. I had been going into the woods to a spot where I became, in effect, a girl, and where I also masturbated. Eventually just sitting there became boring. To add excitement I began walking around in my girl clothes, hoping to be discovered. I wanted to be seen, humiliated, and laughed at by actual girls. I succeeded at this, finding groups of girls at the edge of the woods, near Scout Lake, where there were more homes. The girls almost always laughed once I pulled my skirt up to show off my panties. I masturbated right afterward or, if the situation presented itself, in front of them, which produced even more laughter. I knew this meant I was mentally unstable. My behavior was out of control, and I had developed a supreme guilt complex. One critical thing in favor of my wresting a measure of control over my desires and reckless behaviors was that, except for one isolated drinking experience, I still was not into any kind of alcohol or recreational drug use. That would soon change.

I stole birth control pills from my older sister's dresser drawer. She had so many packets I figured she wouldn't miss a few. The pills contained estrogen, which I hoped could help me grow breasts, add fatty tissue to my buttocks and hips, and maybe even slow down the process of my deepening voice. I wanted to stop what testosterone was doing to me. Nothing seemed to happen at first, but after six months I noticed fat redistribution in my buttocks and hips, and my voice was cracking again, the pill having slowed down the thickening of my vocal chords. I now had two voices: my male one that I used in daily life and my fem one that I used to talk to myself. The range was quite remarkable. As for my more rounded female body, I thought it was perhaps my imagination until one day someone at school said my ass was getting bigger and wanted to know how come. I gave a lame excuse, but now I knew for certain that the birth control pills worked. I loved the feel of my more padded buttocks, flared hips, and how I looked wearing tight jeans or a skirt.

The rage in the fall of my senior year was to get a fake ID. A classmate was taking orders, and I supplied him with a passport-size photo of myself. Two weeks and $50 later I had my ID. I wasn't a drinker but did end up using it to obtain another controlled substance: glue. The glue used to build model airplanes and cars was so potent that it required an adult to purchase it. I had my first glue-sniffing experience at home. While throwing away a bunch of my old models, I ran across a tube of model airplane glue. With the glue and a sandwich baggie I hopped on my Honda 50 motorbike and headed for the woods to change into my girl clothes. Once dressed, I filled the baggie with three squirts of the glue, lay down on my side, and started inhaling. Soon I started feeling dreamy, began hearing odd sounds like a banging noise that must have been my heart pounding, and lost track of time. The high was a complete withdrawal from reality. I excitedly wrapped my right fingers around my penis and began stroking myself. I went faster and faster, breathing deeper, inhaling more glue right as I climaxed. I remained there on the ground for who knows how long, being pretty much unable to move as I waited for the effects of the glue to wear off. Sniffing became part of my routine. I also became curious about inhalants such as gasoline, paint thinner, denatured alcohol, spray paint, ether, other types of glue, and tried them all. Nothing, though, beat airplane glue.

I was increasingly brazen at school, cutting classes left and right that last year. Ironically, I didn't skip class to escape campus but rather to go within it—to sneak into the girls' restrooms and the girls' locker room. Unlike in the woods where I sought out girls, here I tried to avoid detection, positioning myself at the entrance so I could hear if anyone approached to allow myself time to jump up and hide in a stall. I got caught once. I was lying just behind the restroom door masturbating when a girl tried to enter. The door opened slightly. I tried pushing it closed with my left arm but was only partially successful and must have been seen in my girl clothes. The student retreated, but the thrill of possibly being discovered produced an explosive climax and semen went flying everywhere. After my orgasm, I became intensely nervous. What if she was outside the door? I was shaking, uncertain what to do, but knew I couldn't stay in there forever. Slowly I pulled back on the door and peeked into the hall. All appeared calm, so I opened the door further and stepped out. Now my range of vision widened, and I saw two girls sitting at a hall desk. They looked at me with gloating expressions. "Did you like it in there?" one asked, prompting the second girl to demand, "What were you doing?" Even worse, one of them recognized me; we had fought once in the eighth grade. The embarrassment of being caught left me without plausible excuses to offer them. I turned red and slinked away. They laughed, which despite the perilous situation I had just faced instantly turned me on. I couldn't wait to relive the whole confrontation in another masturbation fantasy, and I did minutes later outside the school in a field, out of sight of anyone. It didn't end there. Later that day when school was over, I snuck back into that same bathroom to conjure the whole experience of humiliation and masturbate again.

Word about the incident spread. Students made snide remarks to me about what restroom I should be using. One day in my gym locker I found a pink piece of paper with large, black bold lettering that read "Dubis is a Fem." My former freshman science teacher walked up to me in the hall and sneered, asking aloud how two brothers could be so different, a reference to my younger brother, a rising basketball player. I didn't care that my reputation had reached the teachers. I kept sneaking into both the girls' bathrooms and locker room to jerk off. I kept cutting classes. I kept sniffing glue.

I had a job that year at a store that sold and installed fireplaces. A coworker named Frank, who was a couple of years older, invited me one weekend to come along on a home installation of a fireplace screen. When we got into his car and onto the freeway he lit up a joint. I was surprised that Frank smoked pot because he didn't seem the type. He handed me the joint, and I thought, why not, it couldn't be any worse than sniffing glue. At first, Frank had to instruct me on how to hold the joint and inhale. Several hits later I drifted into another world where I imagined myself in a cute dress, flinging my head back with my long hair, the silkiness of my legs rubbing together, my breasts bobbing up and down, and the feel of lingerie on my body.

Frank interrupted my dreamy state, asking if I was all right. I opened my eyes, realizing we were still in the car on the freeway. I felt incredibly turned on, and the first words out of my mouth were "Where can I get more of this stuff?" I loved how sexy pot made me feel. It was way better than glue, which gave me none of the enhanced feeling of coziness in my body. Frank let me have a joint to take home, which I smoked, masturbating three times and enjoying explosive orgasms each time. A few days later I purchased an ounce of Mexican pot for $15. In becoming a daily pot smoker, I picked up a pastime most of my classmates were already enjoying. Greendale, amazingly, had gone from a quiet backwater void of drugs to hippie central overnight. Everybody at school suddenly smoked pot, and our senior class was the very first to graduate from Greendale High as a class of stoners. Guys grew their hair long and sported beards; girls wore beads and spoke stoner talk. The San Francisco summer of love that happened in the Haight-Ashbury in 1967 and the Jefferson Airplane sound, all that had finally made it to Greendale. It was March of 1972.

I missed a total of forty-two days of class my senior year. My grades were awful, but I managed to hide that from my parents. I had figured out how to erase my grades on the printout sheet and type in a higher grade. Each quarter, I also changed how many days I was absent, so they didn't know I was skipping class.

I met with the senior guidance counselor just once, about a month before graduation. He wasn't at all friendly toward me and asked me very few questions outside of what I intended to do once I graduated. It seemed to me that he was aware of at least some of my "extracurricular" activities and was holding in his anger. After hearing me say that I intended to go to college, he pounced, telling me how such a goal, with the grades I had, wasn't an option. College was for students who applied themselves and had a desire to succeed in life and to be a contributing member of society, he lectured. Not someone like me, he sneered, a person who besides having low grades had also exhibited oddities that weren't normal in society. Besides, he was certain there was no way I could even pass the ACT exam. "You just don't have it in you." It would be far better for me to get out of Greendale, find full-time work in a factory in Milwaukee, settle down, and work on my personal problems, he said. I matched his cold stare and reiterated my plan to attend college before getting up and leaving his office.

In the last weeks of school, I bought my first car, a 1964 Chevrolet Impala, which was dubbed "half-track" because it seemed to go anywhere off the road—through fields, down closed roads, over snow and ice—without ever getting stuck. This car greatly expanded my territory, allowing me to travel greater distances away from home. I quickly filled the trunk up with suitcases of women's clothes and stuffed quite a few pairs of panties and bras behind the back seat. I used the car as a place to masturbate, especially if the weather was bad. I'd drive down a quiet street, pull over, climb into the back seat, and pleasure myself, always trying the best I could to keep a wary eye in case anyone should see me.

Graduation day brought mixed feelings. I was glad to be getting out of high school but upset at the prospect of having to give up the addictive thrill I experienced from entering the girls' restrooms and locker room. Before leaving the house that day, I filled large trash bags with all of my regular clothes, since I intended to move out and live in my car until I could save up enough money for my own place. After packing up my car I returned inside to say goodbye to my mother and explain my plans. She broke down, pleading with me not to leave. I asked why she was so upset considering this was something we both knew would happen. Yes, that's true, she answered, but she pointed out that living in my car wasn't a good solution. She also informed me that a small party had been planned for me after the graduation ceremony and that Dad had bought me a watch. I was skeptical, but Mom seemed so heartbroken, and I couldn't leave her like that. I figured sticking around for the summer wouldn't be so horrible. After I unpacked the car and put everything back into my dresser my mother broke the news that my father wouldn't be attending my graduation that evening. I was not surprised.

The ceremony drew a full house. My class was 350 students strong and smack dab in the middle of the baby boom generation. Stoned as usual, I sat there surrounded by my peers feeling very uncomfortable. I was in choir and at one point had to leave my seat to join the a cappella group to sing our graduation song. Since I hadn't practiced at all, I mouthed the words. During the roll call for diplomas, each student walked across the stage, shook hands with the principal, and received his or her diploma from Mr. Churchill, whom I absolutely could not stand. When my turn came, I heard scattered laughter and jeers, which grew louder with each passing step. What cruel people, I thought, wishing only to receive my diploma and get out of that auditorium. I walked up to the table, shook the principal's hand, and accepted my diploma from a glaring Mr. Churchill. If looks could kill, I would've been dead. I gave it right back to him, my disdainful smirk carrying all the hatred accrued during my years of schooling thanks to so many uncaring and ignorant teachers.

Then it was over. I walked out the front doors of Greendale High never to return again. I felt relief wash over me. As I walked down the hill toward my car, I opened my diploma to see my grades for the four years I'd spent there: several Fs, plenty more grades indicating average and below-average, and sprinkled in were a few stellar marks in history. In fact, I was exempt from taking the final in history my senior year because I had already aced the course. Still, I felt surprised to have graduated. I turned and looked back at the outline of my former high school in the darkness and shuddered. What a chamber of horrors that place was for me, how painful were my four years spent there, and what a waste of time.

San Diego, 1983

It was a gorgeous evening. The temperature was a perfect 70 degrees and a light breeze off the Pacific set the Mexican fan palms swaying as I walked from my car toward my dealer's house with $4,000 in hand, payment for the four pounds of high-grade Thai bud he had fronted me (that is, given to me without payment up front) earlier in the day. Four years earlier I had moved to San Diego from Wisconsin, where I had dropped out of college twice, cycled through a series of jobs, and experimented with a ton of drugs. I had also dabbled in drug dealing, a sideline I picked up again in California.

I was in a good mood. The pot deal had gone down perfectly, netting me $400 for about fifteen minutes of work. Now I just wanted to pay my dealer and get back to my place in Ocean Beach. My plan for later was to snort some crank, Nair my legs and pubic area, change into a garter, stockings, cute panties, with matching bra, a summery dress, wig, do my makeup, and take bong hits all night long. I looked forward to bringing out my props to help stimulate me. These included some still-sealed dominatrix magazines. I would also probably engage in hours of phone sex with a dominatrix somewhere back East, well into the next day, since the crank would keep me up for at least twenty-four

53

hours. If I got really high and brave enough, I might leave my apartment and seek out a local dominatrix. Those meetings were always crazy and involved taking more crank and sharing it, as well as smoking enough weed to sink a battleship.

As I strolled toward my dealer's house with all that cash I had little to be concerned about. Point Loma was one of the safest beach communities in the San Diego area, and my one-bedroom apartment over in North Ocean Beach was also in a very safe part of town. I took a shortcut down a back alley, where, only yards from my dealer's back door, I encountered a group of about six black guys. I was totally shocked, as such a sight was so out of place in cozy, white Point Loma. I could feel panic overcoming me as I approached them. All I could think about was the money, how it wasn't mine and if something were to happen to me—if I were robbed—my dealer would never in a million years believe I got rolled in the alley right next to his house. My fear intensified, welling up so intensely my stomach ached. I thought I might faint, throw up, or both. But then my survivor's instinct kicked in. What had saved me many times in the past came riding to the rescue once again. Power surged through my body. I lifted my stooped shoulders and stood my full six feet. My face became like a steel helmet with steady eyes and mouth creased into a tight line. I cocked my arms in a classic male pose of strength and projected the look of someone not to fuck with. It worked. They all stepped back and I passed by, perhaps because they thought I was carrying a gun.

At my dealer's back door I knocked and in a soft yet urgent voice told him to let me in. The door opened and I dashed inside, warning him to lock all the doors to the house. I explained what had happened, saying how relieved I was that I hadn't been robbed within sight of his home. This guy, sort of a friend, was a complete gun nut. I knew a bit about guns from my childhood, and had a few of my own, but this guy was over the top. He had all types of weapons around his place, from pistols to semiautomatic military style rifles with scopes. Tons of ammunition and gun magazines like *Soldier of Fortune* were everywhere. Being in the midst of a military arsenal helped me relax. The adrenaline left my body and I went limp as I sank into a couch and pulled out the money I owed. Good riddance, I thought, as he pocketed the cash. Now I was ready to smoke a few joints and hang out for a bit before heading back to my place, a world very different from this.

After two hours had passed, I figured there was no chance those guys would still be around. Getting ready to depart, I told my dealer as a joke to "cover me" when I exited his front door. Out of the corner of my eye I saw him pick up a fully loaded HK-223 semiassault rifle made in West Germany and aim it toward the door as I opened it. Suddenly, from the bushes to the right of the door, a black dude, maybe twenty years old, popped out and pointed a .45 Magnum pistol squarely against my forehead and yelled, "Freeze, motherfucker!"

I thought my life was over. All I could think of doing was raising my hands in the air. As I looked into the crazed eyes of this person who was just as scared as me, I simply said, "I'm sorry."

Right as I uttered those words a shot rang out and then another. I was certain it was me who was shot but couldn't figure out why I hadn't gone down. I thought maybe this is how it was just before you die; you didn't really know or feel anything and suddenly you're just dead when you hit the ground. There was a blast of wind down by my left side, up near my raised arm, and suddenly I was jerked back to reality. I hadn't been shot. The dealer had opened up behind me, firing two shots from the HK-223. Both bullets had grazed by my upraised left arm. Had I not put my arms up, the bullets would've hit my side. The guy who had pressed the .45 Magnum to my forehead dove back into the bushes. Then I heard noises indicating the escape of the other assailants through the shrubbery.

Now I had a new problem to deal with. The dealer had slammed the door shut and locked it, leaving me alone with armed assailants possibly staging a counterattack. I ran to the back of the house and pounded on the door, screaming, "Let me in, let me in!" I then shut my mouth, realizing I'd be met with a bullet from the dealer if I kept trying to knock his door down. I managed to calm down by convincing myself the group had fled the scene. Taking a few breaths, I softly knocked and identified myself. The door flew open, revealing the dealer aiming his HK-223 rifle directly at my face. It was the second time I'd had a loaded gun pointed at me on the same night. He too had a bugged-out look and I had to talk him down so he didn't accidentally pull the trigger. Once inside we both stared at each other until I asked him what we should do next. San Diego's finest were certain to show up due to the shots earlier and he had a house full of guns, ammo, weed, and cash. He said he'd handle it. That was good enough for me. I vanished into the summer night, no assailants in sight.

As soon as I arrived at my apartment I checked on my babies, the ten-foot-tall hydroponic pot plants in my bedroom. The metal-halide lamp, or grow light, burned so bright in there it looked like a spaghetti western, with a temperature to match. I located my $50 bag of crank—hard on the nose but worth it for the rush afterward—and chopped out two gigantic lines. Doing crank after nearly being killed twice in one evening probably wasn't the smartest move, but my addictions were very strong and the drama I had been through rationalized getting high. I was determined to make this night work for me yet! I took a few bong hits as the crank started to take effect and grabbed four bottles of Nair that I proceeded to smear all over my body—and I mean everywhere. There was something about being completely smooth that was a major turn-on. I loved to be silky smooth and in my lingerie. The panties, garter, and stockings felt so good against my skin.

Slathering on four bottles of Nair is no easy task. It's messy, distinctly odorous, and gets all over the floor, requiring a lot of towels and washcloths. When rinsing, you can't merely run water over it. You have to take a washcloth and drag it over your body like a paint roller to get rid of all the dissolved hair. It's even worse if you haven't done it for a while, which was the case that night. I had been through one of my periods of trying to fit in, and subsequently my body hair had grown back. I layered on the Nair super thick. Then came the awful part: the fifteen-minute wait necessary for the product to do its thing. Being high on crank helped me handle the burning sensation, except for the skin of my pubic area, penis, scrotum, and anus. This was to be a complete job, the real deal. While waiting I impulsively threw on some lipstick and eye shadow. I knew these cosmetics would wash off in the shower, but I hated being male so much this detail didn't matter. I was in the bathroom and almost ready to enter the shower when I heard the first knock at my door. I tried to pretend I was hearing things. Then a second, much louder, knock reverberated through the apartment.

I tiptoed stark naked, Nair slithering down my body, to the front door, leaving foamy footprints on my cheap living room carpet, and peered through the curtains. Two San Diego cops stood outside. I was furious. The dealer had ratted me out and given them my name. I pulled back a corner of the curtain and attempted to talk to the cops without letting them see any of the white Nair covering my entire body. They insisted I open the door. I told them they had gotten me out of bed and I needed to put on some clothes. I rushed into my bedroom heavily scented by the unmistakable fragrance of the pot plants. No way, I thought, can I let those cops in. I threw on jeans and a shirt and traipsed back to the door, leaving more messy footprints on the rug. By now I was absolutely burning up from the concoction and must've smelled like a vat of chemicals. Because I had once read that if the cops ever come to your door, you should take your house keys and driver's license and step out onto the porch and lock the door behind you, that's what I did.

The pair of cops stared in disbelief, overcome by the powerful fragrance of Nair and the disturbing sight of my makeup-smeared face. I smiled and asked how could I help them. They glanced at each other and then clumsily asked me if I knew anything about guns going off over in Point Loma earlier in the evening. I didn't mince words. I told them exactly what happened—leaving out, of course, the $4,000, the pot, and any link to drug dealing. I described how I had walked by the assailants and noticed them watching my friend's (not dealer's) house and was worried they might be casing it and asked my friend (not dealer) to cover me as I left, whereupon I was ambushed and saved by my friend (not dealer).

The cops insinuated that we were just shooting off guns, but I stuck to my story. Interview over, the good cop said they were not going to arrest me tonight but that I should be available in case they needed to speak with me again. The bad cop said that as much as he'd like to, he wouldn't push things or demand entry to my apartment, although there was probable cause due to the powerful pot and chemical odor emanating from the premises and my body. They said good evening and left. I bolted back inside and straight to the shower. My entire pubic area was chemically burned. It was horrible. As I stood under the shower speeding my brains out, I felt lost, confused, beaten, lonely, and afraid. Why was this happening? All I wanted to do was become a woman. The simple answer was: I lacked the courage to come out. It wasn't my time yet and wouldn't be for several decades.

Part 2

1972–1983

I paid a friend $50 to take the college placement test for me. A week later I got the results in the mail and discovered that "I" had placed in the upper 10 percent of all scores; the door was open for me to apply to any college I wanted. I chose the University of Wisconsin–Stevens Point, and decided to major in forestry. I didn't adjust well to dorm life, discovering to my shock that I was once again surrounded by jocks. I dropped out, moved back home, and enrolled at the University of Wisconsin–Milwaukee, which turned into another academic fiasco because instead of going to class I drove around looking for apartment basements to enter so I could steal women's clothing. I had also resumed my habit of sneaking into women's bathrooms, a practice that now included bathrooms inside churches.

One night I was high on speed snooping around a Lutheran church in Greendale, checking the doors to see if any had been left unlocked. One had. Inside I explored the dark, empty building, coming upon the women's restroom in the basement area. Soon I was visiting this church several times a week, bringing with me a small gym bag containing clothes and panties. My routine was to put on the female clothes, smoke pot, do inhalants, and page through my dominatrix magazines. I would eventually finish, smoke more pot, and begin the whole process over again. I spent hours inside that restroom, sometimes leaving at two or three in the morning, my body soaked in sweat. Sneaking away from the building I would gaze back at the church, which looked foreboding below the moon and the black sky. The scene, coupled with a blowing cold wind, made me feel like a vampire or werewolf running away in a confused, stressful state of mind. It was like a horror dream come true.

Once when I was in the middle of my number, I heard a door open upstairs, followed by soft footsteps. I knew instinctively that whoever had shown up had come for no other purpose than to look for me. I was in the most vulnerable position possible: dressed, smoking pot, magazines open, using my inhalant, lying on the floor in the restroom masturbating. For a few seconds I was motionless. I listened hard to make sure I wasn't hearing things. Once again there was the unmistakable sound of someone walking around upstairs. I calculated that I had just minutes to get out and make my escape through the basement door of the church, which I had earlier unlocked in case of just such an emergency.

In absolute silence I carefully pulled on my outer male clothes, closed my magazines, put everything back into my gym bag, stood up and pinned my ear to the door. Now whoever was upstairs had frozen too, listening for me to make a mistake so he could pinpoint my location. This person knew I was here but uncertain exactly where. Minutes stretched out with excruciating slowness. I had to make a decision. What was the best way to get out of there—a stealthy retreat or a mad dash? Stealth, I decided, held the greater risk because I had no idea yet if this person had already smelled the pot and might be coming down the stairs, closing in on me. There was no choice; running for it was my best chance of escape. I flung open the restroom door. At that very moment I heard footsteps running. Knowing the church layout well, I could tell he was on the opposite end of the building, buying me some time. I threw open the outside door and sprinted into the inky night, crossing an open grassy area toward the protection of the woods. I was the gazelle on the open plains of Africa as I bounded for the safety of the forest. I found a thicket to hide in and I lay down on the cold ground, curling up into an almost invisible fetal position with only my eyes poking out, watchful for any pursuer. It wasn't long before I heard new footsteps, those of a Greendale policeman wielding a flashlight. He came very close, taking care as he moved along, listening for any unnatural sound, alert to any movement, ready for any mistake on my part. I made none and waited a good hour before I crept out of my spot and walked to my car.

Through a part-time job at a sporting goods store I met a guy named Dave who operated fishing camps in Canada. On a whim, I mentioned my interest in fishing and in any related work if a position opened. A week later he called and said there was a job at his fly-in outpost cabin located up in northwest Manitoba. I couldn't believe I was being offered employment in the middle of the wilderness. I quit the semester at UWM to prepare for my imminent departure; I'd be gone the rest of the spring and all summer.

I left in mid-May. My mother packed me a lunch and cried as I walked out of the house. We both knew how messed up I was. Was that the reason for her tears, I wondered, also thinking that perhaps if things were different in my life I wouldn't be making this trip. I was running away from myself. I was a girl forced to be boy and was clueless on how to deal with this. Canada, I hoped, would give me the chance to figure things out. And not just issues related to my gender. I was a college dropout again, felt defeated, and had low self-esteem. I took drugs, had started to drink, wanted to be a slave to women, couldn't date, and was still a virgin at nineteen years old.

My latest set of wheels, a 1967 Camaro, got me safely to Red Lake, a two-day drive. Once there I learned I was stuck, along with everyone else who had turned up because the lake was still frozen and the ice needed to break up before the seaplanes, used there in lieu of nonexistent roads, could operate. Checking in at the local inn, I regretted leaving all my girl clothes behind, hidden in my secret spot in the woods. However, I had chosen to purge myself of my past, a past that part of me knew was impossible to run from. The Red Lake Inn, a decrepit weather-beaten place, seemed like a wayward home for crazies and prostitutes. At three in the afternoon, the bar was already full of drunks: gold prospectors, Mishkeegogamang Indians, bush pilots, resort owners, all waiting for the ice breakup so they could spread out over the province for the summer.

I was told by Dave to look for Poke-um, an old prospector. "Just ask around," he'd said. "He'll be there." Five minutes after entering the bar I was sitting across from him. Poke-um handed me my first Canadian cigarette and filled two shot glasses with Mr. Adams Whiskey Rye. We toasted each other.

I gulped the whiskey, acting like I had done so a million times. Poke-um knew better and laughed. "How do you like that whiskey?" he asked. "Great," I choked out as he poured us each another. He did really look like an old-school prospector with his graying full beard, sparkling eyes, and a grin revealing worn-down teeth. At one point he asked me if I was still a virgin. The barroom had become one big glow, all the many voices blended. By way of response, I laughed, drank more, had another cigarette. In other words, acted like someone I wasn't.

You can hear it." That was how Dave described the start of the ice break to me after he arrived at the inn. He elaborated, describing the initial little popping sounds, then the crunch, at which stage the river would start to move and the ice would crumble into chunks and then move downriver, allowing the lake to open up. "The breakup lasts fifteen minutes," he said. I was excited to witness this but, unfortunately, that year it occurred overnight.

The morning after, the inn's guests hurried off on those seaplanes, dispersing to various points north to prepare for the new tourist and fishing season. At two that afternoon, Dave, drunk, ordered me to get my things. We met at the Cessna, where a bush pilot was waiting for us. Down at the dock I climbed into the back seat of the plane. The pilot—not much older than me—taxied down the river, turned out toward the lake, gunned the engine, and took off. A half-hour later, our plane took a dive, dropping toward another lake. I thought we were crashing, but the pilot was merely landing the plane; we swooped in, gliding like a water bug across the surface of the water. We had arrived at Dave's Long Legged Lake Fishing Camp.

I was assigned to the lead guide, an ancient Mishkeegogamang named Joe, to learn the tricks of the trade. His demeanor and imperfect English reminded me of my grandfather Jaja, who had passed away the year before. I was an eager pupil, confident from my years of fishing in Wisconsin. Every morning I rose at dawn and went out with Joe. He did everything by example and taught me how to navigate the boat through the many connecting channels that led to other lakes, interpret the white capped waves, and drift from one end of a lake to the opposite shore. He explained about the types of lures to use for different depths of water, cutting bait, reading the sky for thunderstorms, getting to shore quickly in the event of lightning, preparing a shore lunch of fresh walleye filets, beans, and bread—which was always a favorite for the fishermen— how to fix an outboard if you had problems, and, most important, how to show a guide's confidence to the others in the boat.

Joe always outfished me. No matter how hard I tried he always caught more walleye pike, northern pike, and whitefish than me. One time we were out trolling for lake trout, moving slowly against the wind and waves, running the outboard ultraslow, and using heavy weights to take our lures a hundred feet deep, where they liked to swim. It was cool and cloudy, with a little rain, and not much fun. I was convinced this was a waste of time when suddenly Joe's rod bent nearly in two and he declared, "I got one." He reeled in the biggest, most beautiful lake trout I had ever seen.

When guests were in camp, my job was arduous. I got to sleep around ten and was up at four. I rarely saw Dave except at suppertime, when he was three sheets to the wind, as he liked to say. He enjoyed acting as the camp entertainer and wore costumes to meals, sometimes dressing as an older woman (hmm, I thought) or donning a suit with a hillbilly hat. He believed the most important thing was to get drunk with the guests and make sure they were having a great time. Our small staff served groups looking for a wilderness fishing experience.

Early on I noticed one of the cooks, a girl from Quebec, often staring at me. I didn't get it at all; I couldn't figure out why she kept looking my way so intently. The mystery was solved one night when I came into the main cabin that housed the bar lounge to check in with Dave about the morning schedule. He was in his hillbilly hat, drunk as a skunk with some guests, one of whom pulled a chair up and invited me to join them. Dave loved the idea of getting me drunk, and I once again found myself in the company of Mr. Adams Whiskey Rye. Somebody offered me a cigar, something I had never tried before. I coughed on the smoke, to the delight of the men. Then, as with Poke-um, the question of my virginity arose. I must've really looked like a kid.

The drinking continued for another hour, when the girl from Quebec appeared and sat down. She looked at me in a sultry way, and it dawned on me that she had an ulterior motive. Feeling the warm glow of the whiskey I smiled at her. I then noticed all the men eyeing me and smiling, so I took another shot of whiskey. Next, I felt a hand reach up under my seat and grab my scrotum and tickle it. The French cook from Quebec had revealed her true intentions! To the laughter of the guests, I made an excuse about needing to check the boats, hastily exiting the bar with the cook right on my heels.

She and I made a quick drunken walk, stumbling through the starlit summer night to her cabin where we jumped into bed. I had absolutely no idea what I was doing, could barely talk, and fumbled with my pants. I climbed on top of her with my pants halfway down and tried to enter her but was flopping all over the place. Only by switching positions did things work. I lost my virginity in a blurred explosion, everything over before I knew it. The last thing I remember before passing out was her telling me she'd had her eyes on me from the very first day of camp.

At breakfast I could barely eat under the inquisitive stares from my drinking buddies of the previous night. When my "first" came in with more pancakes to place on the table, I didn't look at her, even though I knew she was aching for my attention. She was genuinely attracted to me, but I wanted nothing to do with her. I sat there angry at having been so dumb as to have sex with her when now I had to deal with the fallout. I recognized my insensitivity to her feelings yet couldn't help myself.

That night I again got drunk with the guests, who clamored to know if I was still a virgin. When I said no they all cheered, except for one. He spoke up, informing me that the girl from Quebec had the clap. I asked what that was. "It's a genital disease but easy to get rid of," he said. I was told to take a rag, soak it in gasoline, and rub it over my genitals. Taking this cure at face value, I stumbled down to the boathouse and did just that. Within a minute, to roars from the men, I was jumping off the end of the dock into the cold water to relieve the burning pain.

Dave promoted me to a tiny camp on a lake four hundred miles further north, where I was the only person in charge of looking after a handful of high-paying guests. My summer adventure was cut short, however, by an incident in Winnipeg, where I'd gone for a short break. I was riding in a car that got pulled over by the Manitoba police. Though I was tripping on acid, it was the odor of burnt marijuana that got us in trouble. I received a ticket mandating that I exit Canada within five days. Though sad to go, I had grown tired of being exclusively around men. I was thinking more and more of my girl clothes, the soft feel of wearing them, and exploring other ways to become a girl. Clearly, my time away had not changed anything. I was also determined to meet a real dominatrix. I had lasted nine weeks in Canada and, thanks in part to poker winnings, left there with $1,900, a fortune to me.

My first night back in my parents' house all I could hear were the trucks and cars from Highway 36. After the sounds of only nature for the last couple of months, the traffic noise was like a locomotive coming through my bedroom. The next morning I woke up groggy but clear-headed about one thing: I could no longer stay here; it was no place for me. What hurt worst of all was that I couldn't tell my parents or siblings why I had to leave. I was queer, I was tansgender, and a person with kinky sexual habits who wanted to go beyond the borders of not only gender but of normal sexual activity. I wanted to be a girl and a full-time slave to a dominatrix.

I found a small loft in Greenfield, just fifteen minutes away from my parents' house. The owners were remodeling, however, so I was stuck at home a while longer until they finished. In the same week I got a job offer from Pressed Steel and Tank, a company that manufactured high- and low-pressure cylinders for compressed oxygen, nitrogen, propane. It wasn't the job I coveted; not at less than $4 an hour, the starting wage. General Electric, where I had also applied and where my mother now worked, paid more, had a union, was cleaner and more professional. (I did get hired at GE eventually and even become a union steward there. But my own immaturity and drug use would lead to problems and prompt me to quit and ultimately leave Wisconsin for good.)

Life at home in the meanwhile spun out of control. I'd hidden some of my girl clothes under the back seat of my car, where I figured no one would ever find them. And no one did until one day I was struggling to install speakers for a new eight-track tape player, the latest in audio technology for cars. The speaker wires had to be run from under the dashboard and along the doorframe. I was busily engaged in this when Steve, my brother-in-law of two years, pulled up in his car. He was a macho type who turned mean when he drank. It ran in his family. The day of his and my older sister's wedding, his father got into fistfights with guests in the parking lot. At the time I sadly recognized that my sister was marrying someone identical to our father. Steve, seeing what I was doing, said the easiest solution was to remove the back seat. Before I could stop him, he pulled on the seat and out it came, along with my bags of clothes: panties, bras, stocking, garters, dresses. He looked at all of it awestruck. Then he gave me a grin, presuming I was just a normal young man who was having sex in his car with girls. But soon that grin changed into an expression of menace, as he quickly deduced this was something more and now he had a secret about me. It was too horrible. I knew at that moment that every time I saw him from this point on, this unspoken thought would be between us.

In another outing scene, I was moving a bunch of clothes from the basement to my car, and being stoned at the time, I had managed to drop several pairs of panties, which were discovered on the basement stairwell. A few days later my mother said that my father wanted to talk to me and my brother separately. I knew by her tone that it had something to do with finding something that they should not have. I was only wondering if it was connected to drug use, clothes, or both. So it happened that at age nineteen, I had my first sexual discussion ever with my parents over those panties. I denied knowing anything about them, where they came from, how they got there. My brother, I learned, said the same thing; only he was telling the truth. It was left to our parents to try and guess which one of us was lying. The issue was never discussed again, but late one night my mother stealthily entered our bedroom. I had taken to wearing panties almost all the time, even to bed. That particular night, however, I was in regular men's underwear, ugly white cotton ones. I awoke to my mother's presence but pretended to be asleep to find out what she was up to. She ignored my sleeping brother and strode over to my bed, gently lifted the covers to see what I was wearing, put the covers back down, and slipped out. I lay there, eyes open, thinking, so they know! They had talked it over and concluded who the owner of those panties was. I felt deeply ashamed, hurt, angry, isolated, rejected. I was so tired of hiding myself.

The final family incident involved pot. I had several pieces of smoking paraphernalia hidden about, mostly in my car. However, a gas mask with a long green stem that had a huge bowl mounted on the end for stuffing weed into, I kept in the folds of my sister's wedding dress, which was wrapped in plastic and stored in the basement. My mother decided one afternoon to clean the storage area. She moved the wedding dress and the gas mask came tumbling out and hit the tiled floor. Aghast, she confronted my brother and me. This time I admitted ownership. I viewed smoking weed as quite harmless, especially compared to the other drugs I was taking without her knowledge. My mother had a very different attitude. She acted like I had raped a child; she was furious at me for smoking pot and blew up, striking me several times. I raised my fists halfway to defend myself. She retreated in a panic, thinking I was going to strike back, which was never my intention.

My parents and I parted ways in sorrow and sadness. We harbored a hidden anger toward each other and were unable to talk openly—there was a complete gulf between us. After I left, I stopped my car down the road from the house and looked back at the place where I had grown up. I broke down in sobs, grieving at the thought of never again living under that roof. For despite everything, I did love my family. Then, I headed straight to my beloved woods where I gathered the suitcases that I'd hidden there. I cried again as childhood memories of all the times I had spent here came flooding back. This marked the end of an era: my last visit to this special place that had offered me shelter over the years. The leaves on the tall oak, hickory, and elm trees flashed brilliant colors against the bright blue sky. It was like the woods were signaling their own farewell. I pulled my suitcases from their hiding spots in the thicket and I said goodbye, knowing I'd never return. I trudged back to my car, hauling those three large suitcases, portable closets of a secret life whose power I strongly felt yet didn't wholly comprehend.

*W*hen the union position at General Electric came through I became a forklift operator there. My job was to get the skids of materials unloaded from the arriving semitrucks and placed on yellow carts that were magnetized to a conveyor belt. I then tagged the materials with coded cards and used a metal peg to target, via a slot on the belt, where the carts would automatically disembark from the belt, which ran throughout the factory like a giant winding snake. The plant seemed incredibly futuristic to me, with brilliant colors everywhere, a clean sealed cement floor, polished factory assembly stations, a sparkling cafeteria and restrooms, bright and shiny hanging lights. This was radically different from each of my previous jobs that by day's end left me covered in grit and grime.

A big push to get new materials distributed throughout the plant meant plenty of overtime. It wasn't long before I was popping white crosses—the street name for Dexedrine, a type of speed— to help me through the twelve-hour shifts, Saturdays included. I got in the habit of setting my alarm for 3 a.m. to down five white crosses. I'd return to sleep but awaken ninety minutes later, fully alert and speeding my brains out. Without eating breakfast I'd go out into the cold dawn to meet a coworker named Scott at our carpool point. He, too, worked extra hours and popped Dexedrine. We blasted Chicago's hit song "Feeling Stronger Every Day" on the car radio, driving and speeding our young lives away.

One weekend when I had a rare two full days off straight, my brother came by my place with a set of new and very expensive golf clubs, in a fancy new golf bag, which he asked to keep at my house temporarily. Suspicious, I asked where they came from. "A garage," he said. I knew that meant he had been sneaking into open unprotected garages at night and stealing anything of value. I should've said no, but feeling like I had not been a good older brother to him growing up, I gave in. The next day I was returning home from grocery shopping when I turned onto my street and saw three Greendale Police cars outside my flat. My first inclination was to act like nothing was happening, not look at them, and just drive past. Why stop? I thought. I considered driving all the way to the West Coast, which I had been longing to visit. I knew something had happened to my brother and he had ratted me out about the golf clubs. What else could it be? His betrayal infuriated me. How could my own brother give up my name and address to the Greendale Police, my archenemy from so many instances in the past?

More than the golf clubs, I was worried about my women's clothes, magazines, sex toys, several ounces of pot, pipes, a huge bamboo bong, gas mask, all sitting in my loft barely out of sight. But with three squad cars outside my building the ending seemed inevitable. With Sgt. Hayes, a cop I knew from scuffles as a minor, becoming shrill-like as he accused me of holding stolen merchandise, I allowed them to enter and do a search after negotiating exactly what that search would entail. Inside, I pointed to the golf clubs, hoping that would satisfy them and they would leave. But unfortunately the search didn't end there. First they found the bags of pot in the living room along with my pipes. Then they stormed into my bedroom and started rifling through my dresser and closest. It didn't take them long to figure out they had outed a "transvestite," as one of the cops exclaimed loudly, with a smirk on his face. They started pulling lingerie out of my dresser drawers, grabbing my dresses out of the closet and tossing them about, throwing my wigs on the floor. Sgt. Hayes held up a pair of my white men's underwear that I had kept. Handwritten in Magic Marker across the top it said "I'm a girl." He laughed at me, derisively asking, "What is *this*?"

After about two hours of mayhem inside my home, these cops put the pot and pipes in a shopping bag, seized the golf clubs, handcuffed me, and led me down the stairs. They perp-walked me past an overflowing crowd of neighbors to a squad car. I was pushed into the back seat and we drove off with lights flashing and the siren blasting, all of it a ridiculous show. I fought back tears because I didn't want these pigs—that's what they were to me—to see me cry. Why did it matter so much to them who I was? So what if I was different. I was born this way; there was nothing that would ever change that. The squad car pulled up to the back of the Greendale Police Department and I was roughly led inside to be booked for the very first time. They took my photo and fingerprinted me. Then I was put in a cell and left alone; I was not allowed to call anyone. An hour passed and Sgt. Hayes reappeared and took me into a small room where my pot and pipes were laid out on the table. He started asking questions. I denied the pot was mine, said the golf clubs were brought over by my brother and that's all I know about them, and stated that I wanted an attorney. I expected to be further detained, but out of nowhere Sgt. Hayes handed me a citation fining me $225. I was going to be released, he said, and then he informed me he had called my parents to come get me. I couldn't believe that he had involved my parents. I was no longer living with them and objected to this maneuver, strongly suspecting he had done this to tell them what had been found in my place.

The sergeant gave a speech, telling me how sick I was, that I needed professional help fast and that if it were within his power, he'd commit me to a state hospital for the mentally ill. He exited the room, and through a small window I saw my mother arrive. I could just imagine all the information about my secret life Sgt. Hayes was imparting to her. Minutes later he returned and led me out the front door of the station to my mother, who waited by her car. She had been crying, and I felt extremely awkward, not knowing what to say. All I could think of as I got in was to ask for a ride home—to my house, not hers. She seemed relieved that I didn't want to come back with her, and knowing she didn't want to talk about anything we rode in silence to my house. I hopped out, said thanks for the ride, and watched her drive off. Before making it halfway up the stairs I was bawling.

As terrible as this ordeal was, the harassment led me to an awakening, and I realized for the first time in my life that those cops probably had all sorts of things they were hiding from their wives and families. I was a convenient patsy, a target for the hatred within themselves about who they really were, what they really wanted sexually but couldn't have because they lacked the courage to be who they really were. That understanding, which came to light in the squad car, had actually made me smile. Because in that moment I knew the courage was within me to someday come out and be who I really was. I promised myself this during that ride and knew it was only a matter of time before I would be free to be myself. I also got my revenge on Sgt. Hayes in two ways: by pinching some of my pot from the evidence table and later by settling my fine in pennies—Hayes himself had to haul the seventy-five pounds of pennies off to the bank in exchange for bills. My antiauthority spirit first ignited by the nuns was as strong as ever.

One day I ducked into a porn shop in downtown Milwaukee to see what was new inside. I rounded an aisle of magazines and was instantly turned on, as usual. In the aisle I also stumbled upon a book showing a woman standing over a man dressed in panties, bra, and nightie. He was on all fours, with a collar around his neck attached to a leash that the scantily dressed woman held in one hand, while in her other she held a riding crop she was using to spank his protruding bottom. I bought this book as well as several fem-dom magazines, including *Aggressive Women*, which was a favorite. This magazine had recently introduced a section called the "Male Slave Pig Sty" that was devoted to male slaves and invited men to run an ad seeking the dominant woman of their dreams. I became determined to run an ad with my photograph.

Was I really going to take this step? What would I say in my ad? First I needed a photo, so after taking some white crosses, I headed to a photo booth. I wore a plain white T-shirt, but once seated inside the machine I wasn't sure how to pose. Reminding myself this was for the slave section of *Aggressive Women*, I figured smiling was out of the question. That night I took more white crosses, smoked pot, and stayed up writing and rewriting the ad copy. I masturbated, fantasizing about all the dominant women who would soon be writing me, ordering me to a remote city to become their full-time slave, for that was the gist of my ad: pleading to be a full-time slave, promising to do anything for the chance.

I also wrote to dominatrixes who ran their own ads. What a thrill it was when I received two replies. I eagerly opened the first and was shocked at what I read. The sender said that although my letter was appreciated, it would be better for us not to meet, since she knew my family. I could not believe what I was reading until I flashed back to the day I wrote to her, recalling that I had thought at the time that this dominatrix looked very much like one of my cousins. Now I knew she was. So now another of my little secrets was out to someone in my family. I hadn't seen this cousin in years, not since the Christmas Eve celebrations at Busha and Jaja's had ended many years ago. Still, I wondered how I'd deal with this at a family wedding or funeral and whether she would tell my family about my letter.

The second letter was much more promising. Mistress Ann's photo showed an attractive woman with dirty-blond hair dressed in seductive clothes and holding a riding crop. Her short note said that she was a professional dominatrix and wanted me to serve her. I stared at the phone number that could lead me into total servitude and submission. I needed an entire joint to calm down and get into a submissive mood before dialing the number. Three rings and she picked up. Mistress Ann told me she liked what I said in my letter, whose content I had no recollection of, and my willingness to serve. A tribute of $225 was expected for a ninety-minute session. I was instructed to wear panties, garter belt, stockings, bra under my clothes and to report to her the next day at 4 p.m. exactly, not one minute before or after, or I'd be punished severely for my lack of punctuality. I hung up the phone. My ears were buzzing. Even though $225 was a lot of money, over a week's wages, I had no qualms about the tribute to her. I just wanted to serve. It was all I could think of.

That night, in anticipation of my meeting the next day, I took brown and clears—dextroamphetamine—speeding until my bed and pillow were soaked in sweat and smeared with makeup. I fell asleep close to dawn and at 2 p.m. I woke up in a panic. I had less than two hours to be at Mistress Ann's on the north side of Milwaukee. Besides the tribute, I had been told to bring a gift of a certain perfume, which meant another stop. All I had time to do was wash my face. I left wearing the same sweat-soaked lingerie under my clothes from the night before. I was dehydrated, hungry, foul smelling, and exhausted. I popped yet another brown and clear for good measure as I entered a mall. Inside, however, I was unable to find the perfume she'd named. Running out of time, I bought a different brand—probably less expensive than what she wanted. Miraculously, I reached her apartment door exactly at four. I knocked nervously.

"Go back outside," a voice called out. "Wait exactly eighteen minutes and come back."

I returned to my car, smoked some pot, and at the prescribed time knocked again. This time I was let inside. In person, Mistress Ann looked even more beautiful. "Eyes down," she ordered before telling me to get on all fours and present her with the tribute in my mouth that, per her instructions, I had put in a sealed white envelope. She told me to strip naked and said I had better be back on all fours with my nose to the ground before she returned—and no playing with myself, "or else." I asked her if she wanted me to leave my panties on. She retorted, "That's not what I just told you, you'll be punished for asking that" and walked off in her black stiletto boots.

I got back into a doggie position. Though exhausted from being up for almost two days with just three hours of sleep, I was incredibly aroused and badly wanted to masturbate. It took all my will power not to touch myself as I listened to Mistress Ann in the other room getting things ready. I heard metal cuffs being moved about, other restraints, her stiletto boots crossing the wood floor, and occasional laughter. She returned to the room and laughed at me, saying what a good slave I was, but that now it was time for some doggie training. Mistress Ann put a dog collar on me, and then clicked a long leash into place as she began to lead me about on all fours, having first placed a dog bone in my mouth and given me a new pair of panties to wear. We played fetch: she tossing the bone, me retrieving it. "What a fool you are," she said. These words were music to my ears.

That year the women's movement and fight for equal rights had burst into popular culture with the song "I Am Woman," and the lyrics ran through my head as Mistress Ann led me into the other room where I was ordered to again put my nose to the floor with my hands behind my back, which she expertly tied with a soft rope. Sitting on a stool facing me, she began to ask a series of questions: Who is your mistress? Are you my little doggie fool?

Where do you belong? Who do you worship? If I answered anything incorrectly, she used the riding crop on my backside, which she ordered me to keep raised for easy reach of the crop.

She pulled me up by my collar over her knee and pulled my panties down to mid-thigh, got me comfortable on her lap, and began spanking me, first barehanded and then with the riding crop and the English tawse, all the while making me count the strokes and laughing as she told me how my skin was turning crimson. "Thirsty?" she asked next, removing my bondage and leading me on all fours to a dog bowl filled with water and instructing me to lap away like a good little doggie. She was training me. When I finished, she said, "Kennel time for you now, because your Mistress Ann is taking a short break, and I want you to think about things." I was ushered to a dog kennel, urged inside still wearing my leash. Once I was in, she closed the door and put a lock on it. She left me there for ten or fifteen minutes, only to return and remove me from the kennel. Before leaving the room once again, she retied my hands behind my back, saying she didn't want me playing with myself without her permission—which was smart, because that's exactly what I had planned on doing. The room was like a dungeon, with whips, canes, restraints hung in various places on the black walls and burning candles on high stanchions around the room. It was very ceremonial, deep, dark, and mysterious; I felt completely in Mistress Ann's power, wanting only to worship her forever.

Her spiked boots tapped down the hallway. She reentered the dungeon, sat down, untied my hands again, and commanded me to lick the back of her boot heels. "Clean them good." The taste of leather on my tongue thrilled me, and I grew excited at the discovery of a new fetish. "Now do the other," she said. The more enthusiastically I complied, the more encouragement I got. She ordered me back to all fours and to beg her to allow me to kiss the inside of her thigh. My pathetic effort was good enough: she pulled my panties back down, yanked hard on my leash, and guided my face up into her moist inner thighs. I was told to lightly kiss her there. It was my first time between a girl's legs with my face and tongue—and I wasn't sure what to do. Her "kiss harder!" was accompanied by a yank on the leash. "Push your tongue harder," she urged, as she reached over, whipping me harder than before. Suddenly she gasped in pain and pulled my face away, slapping it hard, warning that if I did that again, she'd tie me up completely and beat the living daylights out of me. Obviously, I had gone too deep with my mouth and my teeth must have nicked a sensitive area.

She yanked me back down to paradise, and I resumed my deliberations, determined more than ever to satisfy her to climax, although I was not certain I would succeed, since I had never been with a woman who had climaxed like this. As I slavishly worked to please her, my mind raced. How incredible to be doing this with a woman—to be completely submissive. I thought of other men's first cunnilingus experiences. How many could say it was like this? This theatrical, this compelling, this dramatic! This was art in its purest form, and I was privileged to be a participant in such an extraordinary experience, something very few would dare try. I felt liberated.

The strokes of the riding crop increased to a frenzy, and she wrapped her gorgeous legs tighter about my neck. I felt her tense up and begin to smear her fluids all over me, rubbing her vagina on my face, back and forth, telling me to swallow and be grateful that she was giving me her juices. Afterward, she lay there for a good five minutes, telling me to not say one word, not to move, just keep staring at her holy presence, her Picasso, between her legs. Then I was allowed to lick her clean, which I did, swallowing it all. My reward followed. I was to be allowed to masturbate on the floor, on my side, in her presence, and to come when told to. This would be difficult. I had never masturbated in front of a woman, and even though my mind was very willing, my body was physically, completely spent. I had not eaten, had hardly slept, and had been masturbating almost constantly since yesterday's phone call.

Regardless, I eagerly got to work on the floor as she inched her boots up toward my mouth, at which point she told me to keep stroking myself and lick her boots. She pulled on my leash several times to remind me of my collar and then smashed my face back down on the floor, all the while telling me to keep stroking. I responded to her expert techniques, and her laughter at the small size of my penis further excited me. Finally, holding the leash taut, she warned me to come now or else she would be very displeased and beat me. I exploded in orgasm, coming all over the towel she had placed on the floor. My penis throbbed and drained for what seemed like an eternity, while Mistress Ann stood laughing at my predicament, saying I was a fool for her, that she "owned" me from this point on.

She tossed a new pair of light-purple frilly panties at me. "Wear these the next time I see you." After wiping off my face with a washcloth, she reapplied my makeup and told me to stop at a store, any store, on my way home, and to buy something there to "make sure people see you with your pretty makeup on." This was my punishment for bringing the wrong perfume, and I was to write her a story to bring along next time about what happened in the store. I got dressed in my boy clothes, which reeked with sweat. As a parting, at her front door, she gestured for me to get down on all fours and kiss her boots, slowly and subserviently. I complied and then stood, facing her, eyes down as instructed. She shut the door. The experience was over, but I was hooked.

I didn't end up going inside a store. As liberated as I felt, I was too physically exhausted. It was almost 8 p.m. and I wanted desperately to sleep. At least at the fast food drive-thru I stopped at the girl clerk noticed my makeup and laughed. I was glad that it was a three-day weekend and I was off on Monday. I went to bed as soon as I got home, and woke up Sunday night, almost twenty-four hours later, dehydrated. I was making my way through my trashed flat to the sink when I heard a knock downstairs. I wasn't expecting anyone, but after another knock sounded, louder this time, I quickly washed off my makeup, threw on some clothes and answered the door. A man stood there dressed in a trench coat and a Dick Tracey hat. Was this for real? His outfit and the foggy night made it like a scene from *Casablanca* with Humphrey Bogart. I knew instinctively he was some sort of cop.

Sure enough, he flashed a badge, explaining that he was a Milwaukee vice squad officer. He wanted to speak with me inside his car. Confirming visually the unmarked car at the curb, I froze up. "No way," I protested. I was certain this was a ploy to arrest me for some reason; I had zero trust in any law enforcement by now. He looked at me sharply and said, "We can do this two ways. You can cooperate with me, get into my car to talk, and not get arrested, or you can refuse, and I will arrest you right now, and you will be prosecuted to the full extent of the law for masturbating in women's clothing inside a private apartment building, breaking and entering, and theft. Which would you like to do?"

Once we were inside his vehicle he got straight to the point. He knew I had been entering a certain apartment building, stealing women's underwear, and masturbating in women's clothes. The owner of the apartment building was an attorney who was incensed over what was happening and wanted me prosecuted. There was a strong case against me, the officer said, and what happened next was up to me. If I promised to never again go back to that building, the attorney had already reluctantly agreed not to press charges. The cop produced a written statement that outlined the agreement and told me to sign it or else I would be arrested and taken immediately to the Milwaukee County Jail. Internally I was devastated knowing how close I was to being in serious trouble. But I remained calm outwardly and without any hesitation signed the document, a copy of which was given to me. I didn't even want to read it. Then he said I could leave, adding, "And I hope to never see you again." I looked at him and said the same thing in turn as I got out of that car.

*A*gain I purged everything, keeping only Mistress Ann's panties. I couldn't part with them; my experience with her was too freshly imprinted on my mind. I went back to see her once without an appointment. Surprisingly, she answered, looking as beautiful as ever. I had a vague hope that she might say, "Come in, I want you to be my full-time slave." Instead, she politely explained that I couldn't just show up at her door, I had to make an appointment. She also reminded me that I still had to write the story for disobeying her with regard to the perfume and that she was expecting it the next time I saw her. I returned one final time. I was desperate for her companionship, but she was out of my league. Price-wise, I just couldn't afford her services. I arrived to find her door slightly ajar. Inside, the furniture was strewn about and her clothes and personal essentials were gone; she had obviously moved out. I rummaged around in case she might have left behind panties or other cute items and found a black wig and the English tawse she had used on me. Clutching these I sat down on the floor and started crying. I thought we had bonded, but now I understood that wasn't the case. I was just a client. I cried thinking how dumb I was to believe that she cared for me.

*B*y the time I left Milwaukee, I had plenty of reasons to move away, but it was a drug debt that put me on the road. I headed first to New Orleans, because of a family vacation there in 1969 and a memory of my parents going on a French Quarter nightclub tour and afterward showing me a flyer from one of the venues that read "See the Boys Who Want to Be Girls." I was determined to seek out these clubs and talk to some of the girls there to see if I could get into this scene. I wanted to come out, to elevate my secret life into a regular life. It was time, I thought. That first night, on the power of speed, I gathered up the courage to go into the Quarter. At one spot I went into there was a girl sitting at the bar whom I wasn't sure about but approached anyway. I wanted to know, I told her, if there was a place for me here, right in this bar, to work. I told her about myself, my life, my history. Seeing the desperation in my eyes, she looked right at me and said, "Hon, there are thousands of us here in the Quarter, it's just that nobody knows it. If you really want to do this, you've got to drop the male persona, come out as you are, and be the girl you know that is inside of you. Your blonde hair is lovely. Grow that out even more, start dressing, and have the courage to walk the streets here. Your sisters are everywhere and they will come to your aid, but first you have to learn to walk by yourself. That is the only way."

This oracle had more wisdom to offer: "And this will allow the time you need to see if this is really what you want in life. Being one of us isn't easy in the beginning, but if you find this to your liking, life will open up for you like it never has before, and then one day soon, you can walk back into this bar, get hired, and make some really good money. You're thin, have long legs, a cute face, and would look great in here. But it's you who has to make those first steps all by yourself and there isn't going to be anyone around to help you. The way you just left your home city made sure of that." I sat in a stoned speed stupor and looked at her with wide eyes, hearing the voice of a sage and feasting on the idea of staying in New Orleans and giving this a try.

As I walked through the Quarter witnessing the throngs of revelers enjoying themselves, bar hopping, laughing, carrying on, I now suspected that deep down I simply didn't have the courage.

The next day I was up early and went to a high-end barber shop where I had my hair, complimented the previous night, cut and dyed jet black. I looked like my father when he was in his early twenties. I returned to my hotel room, changed into an expensive suit I'd purchased and lugged my suitcases containing my girl clothes to the airport for a flight to Los Angeles. I had planned for three days in LA before I flew on to my final destination, Honolulu. At the airport bar I had a few drinks and caught the attention of several women. I appeared every bit the young executive. If they only knew what was in my luggage, if they only knew how much I wanted to be just like them.

I never did board that flight to Honolulu, as it turned out. Once in Los Angeles, I stayed in La Crescenta with my Aunt Dorothy and Uncle Frank, relatives I had visited on a previous trip west. I lived in their house almost three months, keeping my suitcases under the bed and never touching them. I never touched them—but my hosts did, I was to discover. One evening I noticed a change in my aunt. Finding me in the kitchen, she showed me a dress she had bought and made an underhanded comment about how I might like such things too, saying, "One just never knows." I surmised that she had somehow figured me out, perhaps by something I let slip while drunk one night—for just like back home, this was a heavy-drinking household. Later it hit me: She had snooped in my bedroom and opened one or both of my suitcases. I confirmed as much when I opened them myself and discovered that things had been moved around.

The following day it became clear my aunt had spoken to my uncle, who suddenly raised the idea that it might be time for me to get my own place. Fortunately, I wasn't without friends, and that night at a bar in the neighborhood I got hooked up with an apartment share. Staggering back to the house in the wee hours, I discovered my aunt at her usual perch at the kitchen table. She was drunk. I smiled and very politely told her I was moving out the next day. In the morning I called in sick to the clerical job my aunt had helped me get, gathered my belongings, and headed over to my friend's apartment. After being shown my new room, I once again hid my suitcases, now inside a closet. I couldn't help but think how the closet was where my life seemed to be stuck.

Soon after leaving my aunt and uncle, and frustrated with my life in LA, I quit my job and hitchhiked south to San Diego, where I knew a Navy guy living off base.

It finally happened. At the age of twenty-five, I met the first great love of my life. Her name was Sheila, and I spotted her thumbing through a magazine in the Safeway where I had begun working.

She was waiting for her girlfriend, Maureen, to finish her shift. Sheila appeared to be using the magazine as a prop to check me out, so I walked by with my shop apron and Safeway name tag, looking every bit the confident journeyman food clerk, and asked if there was anything I could help her with. The next day I asked Maureen about her friend. She said they were going out that evening to a club, and asked if I would join them. I did, and based on the good time we had she invited me a few days later to her place not far from San Diego State University.

Sheila was the first girl I ever told everything to. I opened up because I sensed she had a wild streak in her too. She found the stories and experiences of my life fascinating but full of contradictions. How could I be what I told her yet look so masculine? That was just one of her questions. As we became more familiar with each other, we began to play sex games in which she was the dominatrix and I was the slave. At last I had a girlfriend who was willing to experiment, and I fell head over heels for her, no pun intended. I worried, though, that the feeling was not mutual. Sheila still wanted to play the field, and I was but one of the men she was seeing, a fact that was very hard for me to accept. Still, our time together was exciting. We went to porn shops to buy handcuffs, a leash and collar, and a riding crop, and to department stores to find girly clothes for me. A cute wig, heels, and makeup completed the package.

I brought her my suitcases so she could see my clothes and page through my female-domination, or "fem-dom," magazines. Often we'd go clubbing, get thoroughly trashed, and return to her place to watch John Belushi on *Saturday Night Live*. We'd smoke pot, and then play games afterward. She liked collaring and leashing me, and I loved to be forced between her legs to use my tongue for an hour or more. She got into jerking me off as she finger fucked me, and eventually we progressed to using a dildo. Soon we started to do things in public. She made me wear my collar, though my shirt covered it most of the time. One time during a trip north she used the collar and leash on me on the beach at Big Sur, me walking behind her. We both played dumb about it when a friend with us who had been down the beach but within view asked us what we had been doing.

It tore me up that my love wasn't reciprocated. I became filled with anger and jealousy when I knew she was seeing someone else for the weekend. I could tell that was coming because I'd call her midweek about ideas for the weekend and she'd say she already had plans. I started cleaning her apartment, doing all the household chores and laundry, trying as hard as I could to be a domestic slave. I would show Sheila my waxed legs, arms, and pubic area that without hair made me feel so much like a woman. I got to know her parents a little. She was deathly afraid they'd find out about our unusual relationship. One time her father came to fix something in her apartment, and she had left the riding crop, collar, and leash out on the bed. He had to have seen them, though he never said a word. I was invited to join her parents on Thanksgiving. The night before I decided to try and arch my eyebrows. I totally botched the job, using a razor instead of tweezers. Sheila tried to patch them up with an eyebrow liner, but it was quite obvious that something was not right with my brows. At dinner I kept noticing her parents staring at them as we ate. During that meal it became apparent to me that Sheila and I weren't going anywhere in our relationship. I stopped calling her and began seeing less of her as time went on, slowly falling out of love. Although at one point I had given up speed, I had started taking it again while I was seeing her, and I was also dealing. Occasionally, I would check into cheap hotels on El Cajon Boulevard to be alone and dress and take massive amounts of crank. The drugs freed me from my inhibitions, and on crank I no longer cared what people thought. I never confided to her about my crank use, and following a motel binge I would only approach her again after I had dried out for a week. So while I was able to come out of one closet at least, I was still locked inside another one.

The time came when I could no longer stand being who I was outwardly. This public persona conflicted with the real me, and it could no longer remain this way. I needed help and wanted to come out as a girl but didn't know how. Then a timely story appeared in the *San Diego Union* newspaper about a gender clinic that had opened in Hillcrest, San Diego's gay neighborhood. Hillcrest was located slightly inland from the ocean and right next to Balboa Park, home to the world-famous San Diego Zoo. The article interviewed Dr. David McWhirter, who ran the clinic and was a foremost authority on gender issues. The article explained that the clinic offered services that enabled one to take the first steps towards gender reassignment surgery. I called to make an appointment. First, I learned I'd have to come in and take some tests, which cost money. I said I would gladly pay, and within several weeks I had a date to go in.

The week of my appointment with Dr. McWhirter, I went on a cranked-up bender of epic proportions. The binge spiraled so out of control that I went into a tattoo parlor and had the words "I'm a submissive fool for all women" tattooed across my ass, right above the crack where it could be readable in one line. I wanted all future girls who saw me naked to know who I really was. Being so high, I didn't even feel the ink needle, and my only regret later was not finding a female tattoo artist to do the work. I also went to a beauty salon where I had my brows waxed and my lashes tinted. Then I put on some pink shorts and a top and went shopping at a lingerie store in Hillcrest, feeling the burning on my ass from the tattoo and loving how the girls in the store laughed when I told them the clothing was for me. I went back to my hotel and masturbated for hours, dialing up dominatrixes to tell them about my new panties and tattoo, racking up hundreds of dollars on my credit cards.

When I arrived at the gender clinic I was a complete mess but did the best I could to hide that fact. Dr. McWhirter looked kind, sort of like a benevolent father, and he seemed genuine. He asked a few brief questions and then just sat there smiling. Finally, he said, "Why don't you tell me why you're here." I took that as my cue and unloaded on him, sharing my deepest feelings all the way back to childhood to the crazy days of stealing panties to masturbating in girls' restrooms. I confessed how much I wanted to be a girl, how I worshiped women, and how every time I saw one, I wanted to be one. I told him how my heart ached to come out but I didn't know how, though I knew it was the right thing; I hated being a man and felt trapped in this life that I could no longer take. I told him how I made my money and how trapped I felt in the all-male world of drug dealing. I omitted any mention of my abuse of alcohol, pot, inhalants, and drugs, mistakenly thinking that he didn't need to know any of that.

I held center stage for almost forty-five minutes. After I finished, Dr. McWhirter remained seated staring at me. Finally, he said three words: "I like you." Those words were spoken so genuinely, with such trueness, that I simply smiled back and said, "I like you too." It was then that I first heard about an in-house "screener," Vince Huntington, who would provide a more in-depth analysis of my suitability for hormone therapy and gender reassignment surgery. I was suspicious. I had expected to be a patient of Dr. McWhirter's, with whom I had just shared my life story. Now I was being passed off to a total stranger, a male, who was not gay like McWhirter. My lifelong deep mistrust of men came to the fore, and I replied that I'd have to think about this for a day or two. I left there with mixed feelings but decided the next day that if it took going through this Vince person to get what I wanted, then so be it.

When I returned and met Vince, I liked him despite my reservations. He seemed cool, relaxed, and confident. He didn't try to dissuade me from any of my thinking; indeed, to the contrary, he walked me through the process of how gender reassignment worked, saying that I could begin after a period of time spent chatting with him. I left in a daze; my dream of having a gender change was now within my grasp. When I returned to my apartment and male roommates, I asked myself, Why am I still here? Why don't I get my own place where I can live more openly? I acted decisively and found myself a small studio in Hillcrest. Even so, I would still have to deal with two of my former roommates, Mike and Tom, because of my drug dealing. Dealing was a big conflict for me, as most of my customers were men and I had to be what they expected of me. At this point I was dealing cocaine, and business was booming; Pablo Escobar was in control of the drug trade, and blow was at the height of its popularity in Southern California. I bought a bigger safe to protect my money and soon began to buy guns to protect myself. I ended up with a .45 Colt, a .12 gauge shotgun, and two H&K semi-assault rifles—a .223 and a .308 caliber, each costing me $1,800. Dressed in camouflage gear, I would travel out to the desert with Mike for target practice. And while I was an excellent shot, I slept poorly (though always in my nightie), even surrounded with my loaded weapons. I had my lifestyle and drug use to thank for making me utterly paranoid.

$\mathcal{F}$or the first time since I last lived alone, in Wisconsin, I happily unpacked all my suitcases, putting my girl clothes on display in the closet and stowing my panties, bras, garters, and stockings, all neatly folded, in my dresser. At last I had some privacy. Though this step made me feel better, I was still trapped and not really out at all. In a repeat of the Mistress Ann episode, I responded to an ad in a local sex publication by a woman named Carrie, who wrote that she and her girlfriend, Lisa, were looking to meet "true submissives." I sent off a letter and one day the phone rang. It was Mistress Carrie, with Mistress Lisa right there beside her. They both quizzed me about what being a true submissive was all about. I responded to the effect that worshiping them unconditionally was nonnegotiable and absolute obedience without question was the gold standard. To my delight, I passed their test and was ordered to meet them the next day at a coffee shop in Hillcrest.

Before I even sat down at the table where they were waiting, Lisa told me to kiss her boots. Public humiliation, they warned me, would be one of the ways to train me into obedience. I eagerly got down on all fours to kiss each boot. Next I was told to sit at the table but not to raise my eyes and look at them as we had our coffee and talked. Each time the waitress came by to refill our cups, Mistresses Carrie and Lisa made sure to say something that humiliated me to get a laugh, which was a big turn-on. The pair were seeking an almost full-time slave to clean their apartments, run errands, drive them around, and be available for whatever random needs might arise. In return I could expect to be trained properly in becoming a "sissy maid": learning the art of being the perfect maid in all aspects. I also would be trained to properly enjoy being humiliated and be allowed, on rare occasions, to worship their feet, shoes, boots, and vaginas, and to perform in front of them on command. Disobedience would not be tolerated in any form, and a variety of punishments would be employed as needed, ranging from over the knee spankings, restricted bondage, the use of a riding crop, or other means. If I failed in my new role, banishment would be the end result. They could always find someone else to serve them, I was told.

That evening Carrie put me straight to work cleaning her apartment. They had a tiny bell to summon me, and I would enter the room on all fours, dressed in my newly purchased maid's outfit, complete with panties, stockings, and heels, as well as a wig and makeup that they had lavishly applied. After several hours of cleaning, scrubbing, and dishwashing, I was allowed to kneel in their presence while they verbally reviewed my work. Mistakes were made, they said, and for that I was forced to spread my legs, panties pulled down, and submit to being spanked with riding crops until they saw the exact shade of red they wanted. They loved my tattoo, could not stop laughing, and assured me there was plenty of room on my ass for additional writing. After my punishment I was collared and leashed as Mistress Lisa slowly yanked me like a puppy toward her vagina, where I spent the next fifteen minutes being trained on how and where she liked my tongue. Then after wiping my face clean, she handed me over to Mistress Carrie for the same drill. I was finally allowed to masturbate lying on the floor and made to stare at their boots. Mistress Carrie at one point made me put my fingers over my lips and twiddle them while humming. I had an explosive orgasm at that moment and was promptly punished with a hard hand spanking. The infraction? Coming without permission. I was sent home in my maid uniform and told to stop by the 7-Eleven and buy a candy bar with receipt as proof that I had obeyed their instructions. Unlike the time with Mistress Ann and the wrong perfume, I fulfilled this command without hesitation.

The two new mistresses ended up not only upgrading my girl clothes but also my boy look, taking me to chic gay men's clothing stores and outfitting me with colorful tight slacks, shirts, and shoes—gone were the boring jeans, T-shirts, and tennis shoes. They took me to get my hair permed and my brows waxed for a more shapely, feminine arch, which I loved. Underneath my new clothes, I was instructed to always wear panties and a bra; I could keep only two pairs of boys' underwear strictly for an emergency. My new style was considered "gender neutral," and I was petrified of being seen dressed like this outside of Hillcrest.

In fact, a fair number of my drug customers, usually those with more disposable income and a higher level of education, complimented my appearance, although there were funny stares whenever it was obvious I was wearing a bra. I realized it really didn't matter what I looked like; customers only cared about how much blow I had and how good it was. My relationship with Mistress Carrie and Mistress Lisa continued, and there were occasions when I spent time with them separately at their respective apartments. Whenever either would call me, I had to drop whatever I was doing and immediately respond to them, giving them what they wanted, which could be something as simple as bringing fresh coffee or an hourslong house-and-vagina cleaning. Sometimes my devotion to them interfered with my drug dealing, but not nearly as much as it would have before meeting them. Since meeting the pair, I had eased off the crank and limited myself to pot and alcohol. I bought a wine cabinet that held up to 120 bottles and began stocking it with fine wines, including Château Latour, Château LaFite-Rothschild, and rare white vintages.

My younger brother, who had moved out to Southern California soon after I did, was all set to get married. I agreed to be the best man but was uneasy over how I would be viewed by my parents, who were flying out, along with other relatives. I had changed so much from my Milwaukee days—even from my La Crescenta days. Booze offered a solution, or at least one way to feel safe. The day of the event I loaded up my car with six cases of wine, intending to get as drunk as possible and hoping my relatives would too. My brother was marrying into a wealthy family and I took an immediate dislike to his future father-in-law, whom I could tell was not happy with these Polacks showing up, much less the prospect of his baby daughter marrying one.

The ceremony went smoothly, but I struggled to act normal at the reception, held at the mansion of the bride's parents in Corona del Mar. I felt very uncomfortable around my parents, not knowing what to say to them. It got so bad that I phoned Mistress Lisa and begged her to hop in a cab and come to the reception to be by my side. She agreed, and the $250 cab fare turned out to be worth every cent. Soon I began cracking open the cases of wine, spreading bottles about. The wine was far superior to that being served, a fact that drew an angry look from the father-in law. At one point, Uncle Frank even stood up and toasted me, declaring, "Now there's the Ernest Hemingway of the family." I held my wine glass high and smiled broadly, thinking, boy, if he—no, they—only really knew. Mistress Lisa, who did know, winked at me. Our closeness prompted Aunt Dorothy, who had been closely observing us as she drank steadily, to ask my date, "So what do you for a living?"

Mistress Lisa replied, "I'm a taxi driver."

"A what?" my aunt said, shocked that a woman would drive a cab.

Uncle Frank chimed in with a roaring laugh, saying, "A taxi driver! That's great. How do you like driving a cab? Meet a lot of interesting people I bet." That pretty much shut down my Aunt Dorothy. As the night progressed, I hauled out more wine, putting it in the middle of the action for anyone to grab.

At the next morning's late breakfast I got some shocking news. I had asked my parents what was next for them during their visit.

My mother told me they planned to do some sightseeing in LA, after which Dad intended to come back down to San Diego and spend time with me at my place. *"What?"* I blurted. I must have misheard, I told myself. Did she just announce that my father was coming to visit me and stay at my crummy studio apartment that was loaded down with cash, cocaine, pot, Quaaludes, inhalants, girl clothes, wigs, makeup, fem-dom magazines, S&M toys, and a phone that rang constantly with customer calls for drugs? Mom calmly replied that he'd be spending a week with me, saying that this was a good time for us to become reacquainted as father and son. "He's looking forward to this, so please don't say no," she added. I was too dumbstruck to argue. How was I going to deal with my father for an entire week, someone I disliked and who, at critical moments of my life, had shown open contempt and hatred toward me? How was I going to hide my business from him, my lifestyle, my ringing phone? The way this was being foisted on me felt utterly unfair, and my first inclination was to reject it out of hand. In the end I relented because I would have a three-day head start on him, time to get my apartment ready. I also, reluctantly but hopefully, took my mother's words about reconnecting with my dad to heart.

I repacked all of my girl clothes and magazines into suitcases, which I hid in the trunk of my 1975 Lincoln Continental, a car I took in lieu of a drug payment and that served as a backup to my new VW Rabbit. It was a real ghetto car: bright gold, white vinyl top, leather seats, spoke wheels, all-power everything. I moved my cocaine, pounds of pot, and fifty thousand Quaaludes to Mike's house; he understood perfectly my situation. In order to make my rounds, I wrapped a smaller day supply—several pounds of pot, eight ounces of blow, and five thousand Quaaludes—in plastic and stuffed it a small cooler that stayed in the Lincoln. The last problem to solve was the phone. I considered just unplugging it whenever I left the house and my father was home alone, but then instead I bought a Phone Mate answering machine, which I could access remotely from a pay phone. For that period, the technology of my new Phone Mate was amazing. I was now as ready as I'd ever be for my father's visit. My plan was to get up each morning and leave the apartment, claiming I was off to work at Safeway when really I'd be spending the day distributing fronts and collecting money from the previous days' fronts.

It was one of the strangest weeks of my life. I'd return from "work" to find my father waiting for me. And for what? Even small talk was awkward. One night I took him to Pacers, San Diego's premiere strip joint, thinking he would like that because he used to always check out women when I drove around with him as a child. After two drinks, the minimum, he was ready to leave. Another night I took him to dinner at El Indio Restaurant, a famous Mexican spot. As we were driving home in the Lincoln, he pointed to a gas station. "That's a nice-looking gas station." In the moment I thought it was an absurdly meaningless statement. But later I figured out this remark had been his way of attempting to have a conversation with me. We had so little in common, so little to talk about. There was an iron curtain between us.

I kept a therapy session that week with Vince, who wanted to meet him. Bring him in, I was told. I couldn't bring myself to oblige the request. Were my dad to know I was in therapy at a gender clinic, it would end our relationship, limited though it was. On the way to the airport, my dad mentioned the phone, saying it sure rang a lot, adding that I must have a lot of friends. He was no idiot; did he suspect something? I wondered. I dropped him curbside, where we parted with a quick handshake. As he walked into the terminal I waited to see if he might turn and wave, but he didn't. I got back to my place and bawled like a child. There were so many things I wanted to tell my dad but couldn't. How could I tell him what I did for a living, and how could he ever understand that he had a son who wanted to become a woman? How could he ever understand Mistresses Carrie and Lisa? I recalled the comment about the gas station and cried even harder, thinking that was when I should've told him that I loved him and always would. That was the moment to move beyond the past and I didn't seize it.

$\mathcal{A}$ momentous day arrived for me: Vince declared I was ready to begin hormone replacement therapy. He knew everything about me at this point, including what I did for a living. In fact, I brought him a few grams of pot every once in a while as a gift. It was always so cute to watch him roll the baggie up very tightly and place it inside his dress sock. Vince's announcement about hormone therapy surprised me. I had struggled with his repeated attempts to convince me to consider alternatives to a sex change, all to the point where I had began to wonder whose side he was really on. Yet now he had come around. An appointment was made for me to meet with the only medical doctor in San Diego who was willing to prescribe female hormones to a male.

This doctor turned out to be a no-nonsense individual: very dry and not very friendly. Though Vince had warned me in advance about his manner, it still rubbed me the wrong way. I was given a hospital gown to change into and left in a cold waiting room for an interminable amount of time, or so it seemed to me given my wicked hangover that day. After a physical, I was handed a stack of papers with detailed questions about why I wanted a sex change and was given only a limited time to answer them. I had expected a prescription to be issued but none was and I left feeling deflated and disappointed.

A week later I went to my therapy session upset that I hadn't heard anything from the medical clinic. Well, it turned out that the doctor, after getting my blood work back, had called Vince to tell him that he felt I was not a good candidate for hormone replacement because I had a high alcohol content in my blood, and, moreover, I had seemed severely depressed. He did not want me on hormones under these conditions. I blew up, telling Vince the doctor had no right to play the role of a psychiatrist because that was the job of the gender clinic. He said there was nothing we could do outside of refocusing on my issues and maybe finding another way, meaning an alternative to gender reassignment. Angry and upset, I considered locating a doctor in Tijuana who would prescribe me female hormones or, even better, a pharmacy there where I could simply buy Premarin, the best estrogen on the market. After calming down, I elected to play it the way Vince wanted, agreeing to work with him and not change the plumbing. He was very supportive, promising to go through things slowly, deliberately, and thoroughly, getting to the bottom of my issues so that I could become the well-rounded, centered person he knew was inside me. Which sounded great, only I still wanted to be a girl. Nothing was going to change that.

I joined a group that Vince put together for male cross-dressers. Try as I did, I couldn't come to terms with the ultimate objective of the group, which was to deny me a sex change. I grew weary each week of hearing these men complain about their lives, how cross-dressing was where it was at, and how having a sex change wasn't. Soon I dropped out of the group and stopped seeing Vince altogether. I also dropped out of San Diego State University, where I had been taking classes sporadically. Giving up my goal of getting a degree when I had close to ninety units and some very good grades was a blow to my self-esteem. Only the drug dealing continued. Selling drugs was the one thing I was successful at. Even this was questionable. For while I was making money on paper, many people owed me money. I fronted customers just to get a partial payment, leaving them with cocaine and a bigger debt I worried would never be paid back. It was a losing proposition that came to a head one day when Tom came to me needing pounds of pot, which I procured for him. Only then he refused to pay up, saying he needed to clear his books with me, because I owed him money. I'd been hoodwinked and there was nothing I could do except go to the supplier in the deal and set up a payment plan.

$\mathcal{M}$istress Carrie and I were driving downtown late at night. I had on full makeup, pink shorts, a panty set that included a padded bra, and a long black wig that I loved. There was a photo on my shirt of a slave in a hood cover, his genitals tied up, with a caption that read "I'm a slave." Our first stop was a porn store. I walked the required five feet behind, eyes down, as we entered. Mistress Carrie selected several riding crops, a ball gag, and a delicate cane, items I paid for of course. For the walk back to the car she attached the leash to my collar, and with my eyes cast down, I heard people on the sidewalk laugh.

I didn't see the car that ran a red light and plowed into us. It must've been several minutes after the impact when I opened my eyes to behold fire trucks and cop cars swarmed around us. I thought I was dreaming—until I felt an intense pain at the center of my chest and I heard Mistress Carrie groaning. A fireman told me not to move, saying they were working to get my car door open. Meanwhile, they helped get Mistress Carrie out on the passenger side. She asked to go to the hospital and was immediately put in an ambulance and driven off. The first responders finally succeeded in prying open my door, and there I was in all my slave-attired glory. Clearly I was not what they expected, and they looked freaked out, unsure how to handle me. I was in too much pain to care what they were thinking. I was also speeding my brains out. I stared at my VW Rabbit, its driver's side totally smashed in, and then saw the car that hit us. It was a large Cadillac that appeared barely damaged, though smoke was coming out of the engine area. Apparently, the driver had run off on foot after hitting us.

A policewoman approached and asked me questions. She urgently wanted me to go to the hospital in an ambulance, but I steadfastly refused, insisting I was fine, even though I was in incredible pain. "Can you take me home?" I whimpered. After I refused again to go to the hospital, she relented and told me to get into her squad car. I mentioned that I needed to first retrieve something from my car. She said all right and I walked in my heels past all the gaping male cops, opened the hatchback, leaned in while enduring chest-stabbing pain, grabbed the Igloo cooler, and paraded again past the still-staring cops to the squad car. The policewoman began driving. What she didn't know was that my cooler contained two pounds of pot, ten ounces of cocaine, Quaaludes, and cash. She pulled into my carport and helped me to my back door, even carrying the cooler. Once she had left, I collapsed onto the kitchen floor.

Unable to stand, I crawled to the phone and called Ed, a former roommate who was an attorney. While grateful not to need his professional services that night, as a friend who knew me well and knew the life I was leading, I longed for his company after this close call. It was two in the morning, but he agreed to come over right away. Before he arrived I changed back into boy clothes, an agonizing effort because I couldn't bend over and was having trouble breathing due to the excruciating chest pain. It was enough to ask him to come at that time, and I worried that the slave getup might alienate him.

Eventually, I did seek medical attention and I was diagnosed with a severely sprained sternum, the result of being pushed into my car's steering column. Ironically, I was told later that the guy who hit me was caught by the cops and his car was found to be loaded with drugs! I spoke with Mistress Carrie once by phone after the accident, calling her to see how she was recovering from her severe whiplash. It was a brief conversation; the accident had spoiled our friendship. On a sunny afternoon weeks later I saw Mistress Lisa as I was driving in Hillcrest. She was walking, and I honked to get her attention. We ended up having coffee and chatting. She let me know she was leaving for Australia in a few days. It wasn't a big surprise. Before we first met, she had just returned from living in Manila for a year. She asked if I remembered anything I had written in the original letter I sent to her and Mistress Carrie. She said she wished she had it with her so I could read it. Her point was that no one could ever be the kind of slave I aspired to in that letter. It was impossible because being human, even the most devoted slave with the best of intentions has self-interests that can prevent him from realizing his fantasies. She told me that afternoon how she and Carrie had agreed to see me because they saw my intent, coupled with desperation, and wanted to give me a chance. There was more that had impressed them. My letter showed a human side that they felt was genuine, which more than anything led to our meeting. Then she leaned over, kissed me on the lips, got up and left.

*D*ue to my generous program of offering fronts, and my negligence in collecting, the number of people who owed me money was out of control. One person, Rick, owed me eight grand. But every time I went to his house, he had another excuse why he didn't have the money. I knew deep down that he would likely never have the money. I was desperate to recoup from those whom I had fronted in order to pay those who had fronted me.

This vicious cycle was about to lead me into a grave trap.

A customer named Al introduced me to two buddies who said they could move large amounts of cocaine up in LA if I would be interested in working with them. Trusting Al, I said sure. Not long after this talk I got a call from the pair, asking if they could come over and buy an eight ball, slang for 3.5 grams of cocaine, or an eighth of an ounce. When they arrived, Al formally introduced me to Brian and his "friend." As we sat around talking about business, I noticed that Brian's friend never said a word, which I found odd. I told them the blow came from Tom, who also had thousands of

Quaaludes. I bragged about having done hundreds of thousands of dollars worth of business with Tom, my former roommate. When I brought out the eight ball, they keenly checked it out but declined doing a line, saying they could tell by just looking at it that it was good stuff. They paid me $350 in crisp, new bills and then split. Days passed without a word from them. I wondered what had happened, and when Al stopped doing business with me, I picked up the phone. I asked him if everything was okay and when we could expect to do more business with his contacts up in LA. He reassured me that things were cool and that sales had just cooled off temporarily.

Becoming impatient, and needing the money, I finally called Brian directly. I asked him how he had liked that eight ball. "It was fantastic," he told me. That got things rolling; he started asking about quantity—how many kilos of cocaine could I pull together, and how much would it cost? I was cautious about speaking on the phone and asked if he would like to meet for coffee. He immediately agreed and we arranged a time for the next day. I hung up, excited about the kind of money I could make if I started selling whole kilos of blow. I'd finally settle my debts, be free and clear.

That night I went over to Tom's condo in Point Loma; I needed to make sure he had the volume. It had been a while since I'd seen him, and while I looked quite different, he didn't care; there was too much money at stake to worry about personal appearances. I ran the whole thing by him. He said he was into it but first wanted to meet with Brian and me. My plan had been to keep Tom out of the actual deal; if he became too acquainted with Brian, what would I be needed for? He could just start selling cocaine directly to Brian, cut me out after the first go around. Tom reassured me that I'd always be in on future deals but that since we were talking about kilos, nothing could really be done unless he met Brian.

When Brian surprisingly agreed to meet Tom, I worried about him getting too comfy with my connection. The whole thing was unraveling, and I was not a happy camper when I introduced the two at a coffee shop. Brian took the lead, putting me at ease by saying the three of us were a team. He complimented Tom on the quality of the eight ball sample. I sat there having visions of millions, about where I'd retire in a year or so . . . Mexico perhaps.

Tom suggested starting with a smaller amount, perhaps one kilo to see how things went. Brian pushed for more, saying he had all the cash and a larger amount would mean all of us making more. Telling us to think it over, he got up and left. After discussing the options, Tom and I agreed to offer one kilo of blow for $100,000. After three days I phoned with the terms, but only got an endlessly ringing phone. For the next several days it was always the same result: no answer. It was strange that Brian had become inaccessible considering how keen he was on this deal. Then finally he answered his phone and I went over the details, talking in code, saying I could have a "package of one" ready whenever he wanted and explaining how this would serve as a test run for "future jet landings" with "more planes." I arranged for the deal to happen at my house, since I still had the feeling that I was going to be cut out of the action. I was doing everything I could to be a player. Really, I was only the middleman; it was Tom's blow and Brian's cash.

The evening of the buy got complicated quickly. Brian told me by phone that Al would come over first to verify that we had the package, and then I was to follow Al outside to a car where Brian's friend, whom I had only ever met at that first meeting, would show me the $100,000. "Why all the cloak and dagger?" I asked. He responded that it had to be done this way because we were new working together. I communicated all this to Tom, who said he'd be right over. But Tom arrived with his own plan. He pulled out not one but two kilos of cocaine: one fake kilo and a real one wrapped in cellophane with a big ribbon tied around it. I stared at what looked like a birthday present. The idea, he said, was to have Al come in, see the real cocaine, leave with me to the car, at which point he would hide that kilo and put the fake kilo out on the coffee table for viewing.

This ploy would protect us in case we got robbed. If a gun was stuck in our face, he said, we could hand over the fake kilo and let them leave. All this hush-hush stuff was wearing on me, and after passing Tom a beer and two Quaaludes, I swallowed three and opened a fresh beer for myself. At least I had the perfect hiding place for the real kilo of blow. After a near robbery months earlier, Al had installed an electronic trap door inside my closest that accessed a metal box that could hold plenty of drugs and cash. He had installed a red warning light in the corner of the closet that would trip and blink if someone unauthorized entered into my bedroom without first turning off the secret cutoff switch. It was an ingenious system and I was glad to have it for this special occasion.

Finally, there was a soft, almost inaudible knock at my back door. I opened it and there was Al. A chill ran through me; he seemed unusually nervous as I led him into the living room and straight to the kilo of blow. Tom unwrapped it and Al dipped a finger into it, tasting it and saying it was great. As planned, Al led me outside to the parked car, telling me he would get Brian and meet me back at the house. I was left alone with Brian's friend, whose name I didn't even know. As this guy opened a briefcase on the front seat to reveal neatly stacked bundles of $100 bills, a truly creepy feeling overtook me. I picked up one and thumbed through it, nodded my satisfaction, and got out of the car. En route back to my place, a strong suspicion overcame me that the "friend" was an undercover cop. The way he had looked at me, with his cold hard stare and a face filled with hate. I'd experienced that look countless times in my life. My whole body began tingling and my mind started screaming, run away! Which, in fact, I was prepared to do. In anticipation of tonight's deal I had parked my car away from the house. In the glove box there was money and my passport.

I had my car keys on me, so I could've acted on my instinct. But I didn't. Inside my apartment, Tom was sitting there with the swapped fake kilo of cocaine on the coffee table, the real cocaine hidden away. My fears fell away, and we awaited the arrival of our guests so we could commence the deal.

Time went by, more than expected. I was tempted to take another Quaalude but the three I had already taken were making me slow, although that sluggishness was tempered somewhat by the adrenalin pumping through me over this impending payout, in which I stood to make $3,000 instantly with the promise of more in the future. Again there was a soft knocking on the back door. I smiled broadly at Tom, who clapped his hands, saying, "Here we go, it's show time!"

I unlocked the three deadbolts before turning the doorknob and opening the door. Instead of finding Al and Brian, there were three guys who looked like hippies standing in crouched positions with guns pointed at me. At the same time I heard a commotion in the living room—the front door was being broken down. The hippies stared at me like they were totally zoned out on crank; I was certain we were being robbed. They screamed at me to lie down and one hit me over the head with a club, sending me down to the floor, where I felt handcuffs placed on me. A badge was shoved in my face. "We're the San Diego Narcotics Task Force," the hippies screamed, "and you're under arrest." *Cops.* My intuition had been right.

They dragged me into the living room, where Tom was already handcuffed and sitting in a chair with two cops guarding him. All the police were in plain clothes; I didn't see one uniformed cop anywhere. One of them showed me a search warrant, screaming at me to read it out loud. I refused, saying I wanted an attorney, since I was under arrest. This only infuriated him further. Screaming into my face, he read aloud the part of the search warrant saying they were there to confiscate cocaine.

Just before the cops arrived, Tom had moved the fake kilo into my bedroom, placing it under the blankets on my bed. Now the cops fanned out into each room, tearing through everything. I heard dishes breaking in the kitchen. Then I heard a cop announcing, "We've got a dink here," as he laughed hysterically. The term wasn't familiar to me, yet I knew they had found my girl clothes and other things. There was more laughter as they paged through my dominatrix magazines, exactly like so many years ago when the Greendale police had searched my loft. History was repeating itself, only this time it wasn't over a paltry set of stolen golf clubs.

A scream, almost a howl—like something out of *The Hound of the Baskervilles*—reverberated throughout the apartment. A cop had found the fake kilo of cocaine in the bed. The others all piled into the room. Suddenly finding myself unguarded I contemplated bolting out the front door, which was still wide open. I could smell the sweet summertime night air of San Diego and knew this was my last possible chance to escape. Convinced the authorities would try and lock me away for a long time, I began to rise out of my chair in an attempt to run, but then sat back down. There were bound to be other cops outside the house. Even if not, I was handcuffed and would scarcely make it fifty yards. I began to think about prison. How would I survive? My ass was covered with tattoos that told anyone what I was about. Not only that, I was wearing a bra and panties under my clothes and knew that a strip search was in my near future.

A loud chorus of ooohs and aaahs signaled to Tom and me that they had unwrapped the gift-wrapped package. My spirits lifted. Once they figured out it was fake, they would resume searching for a real kilo, but there was chance they might not find it. Maybe I would not be taken in: no blow, no jail. I heard a cop call out for the test kit. Silence followed, except for the crinkling sound of the cellophane wrapper being further pushed back. Seconds later, a scream: "It's fake!" The cops buzzed out of my bedroom like angry hornets. Two got down in my face, shouting, "Where's the cocaine, dink—*where's the cocaine?*" I calmly asked the most berserk cop, who couldn't stop spraying me with spittle, if he had a speech impediment because he was spraying all over me, adding that I had no idea what any of them was talking about. After a pause the cops resumed their wanton thrashing of my place. They were moving away from, not toward, the safe. My hopes soared.

Now for the first time Brian made an appearance. After he flashed his NTF badge at me, I knew for certain that Al was involved in this bust and had been from the very beginning. How could he do this to me? What was his motivation to ruin my life completely? The world seemed to be turned upside down. Then I shuddered, remembering it was Al who had made and installed the secret stash area behind my closest.

*B*rian asked me to cooperate and tell him where the cocaine was. If I did, he said, things would go easier for me. I couldn't believe that Al would have not told him about the safe. I just looked at Brian and said I had no idea what he was talking about and reiterated that since I was under arrest, I had nothing more to say and wanted an attorney. Meanwhile, the cops were still laughing at all my clothes, tossing them everyplace. Things soon quieted down until a uniformed officer came in with a drug-sniffing black lab, which made a beeline for the bedroom. The dog scratched at the closest wall and inadvertently tripped off the red blinking warning light. The cops went nuts, afraid the place might be booby-trapped. For a moment I thought about lying and saying it was, wagering they would panic and run, allowing me to escape to my car. Instead, I looked around at these macho pigs and said, "I thought you were all so tough and brave. Don't you want to die for your big bust?" Then I laughed and put my foot over the pressure plate, which tuned off the red blinking light.

They took a hammer and smashed in my closet wall, and then pulled out the real cocaine. A test was run again. This time they exclaimed with joy at how pure, how good it was. Brian hadn't forgotten about the fifty thousand Quaaludes, which the cops retrieved from the carport utility closet. Their haul also included three pounds of pot, cash, and a loaded shotgun. These wacko cops next tried pumping me and Tom for information, asking questions about where we got the kilo of cocaine, telling us things would go smoother if we cooperated. I repeated that I wanted a lawyer. Being the middleman in the deal, I was hopeful that would mean a lesser charge.

The NTF led Tom and me out to a regular squad car and shoved us inside. On the freeway I watched the city lights pass, fear eating away at me as prison loomed. One cop mentioned how lucky we were to be going to the Metropolitan Correctional Center, or MCC, a federal facility, and not the regular county jail. I tried to take solace in this, for I was desperate for any shred of hope. We were taken underneath the federal building and from there inside to be booked. I was told to put all my clothes in a bag and was left standing naked with my tattoos on full view. Next I was forced to bend over, open my mouth, tousle my hair. They gave me an orange jumpsuit to wear, as well as plastic sandals. I was fingerprinted, photographed, issued a federal inmate identification number, and interviewed by a nurse. "I want to kill myself as soon as possible," I told the nurse in no uncertain terms. "I'll do whatever it takes to make that happen." My ulterior motive was to be placed in solitary confinement—anything other than being placed in the general population.

Those magic words worked. Unlike Tom, who was sent to a large, populated cell, I was placed in an individual one. Although it was 4 a.m., I demanded that I be allowed to make my one phone call. Several hours later I was led out to a phone, which I picked up to call Vince. I was so lucky that he answered. As soon as I heard his familiar voice, I couldn't help myself and began crying. The first thing Vince told me was that we both knew that this could happen someday, reminding me of how we had talked about what had now come to pass. He asked what he could do, and I asked him to call Ed to represent me at the arraignment hearing in federal court later that morning. Vince said he would do the best he could and hung up.

After being led back to my cell I collapsed. Never before had I felt so alone and helpless.

Oregon, 1997

As usual the mountain road had very little traffic. I was returning home after leaving Reba, a family cat, for overnight supervision at the vet's in Saint Helens, a town on the Columbia River. For the long drive I had plenty of help. In the cup holder of my pickup sat a forty-ounce bottle of Rainer Ale, a local malt liquor nicknamed Green Death for its high alcohol content. This was my third. I also had good weed packed into a glass pipe. By steering with one knee, I could raise the pipe to my lips for a quick hit. But performing this maneuver now, I headed into a sharp, downhill curve faster than I knew was safe.

Rounding the turn I feared the presence of an approaching car and slammed on the brakes, dropping the pipe and jerking the steering wheel to the right. The exact wrong combination: I suddenly felt the entire truck go airborne. Inside the cab, a centrifugal force slammed me against the ceiling as my hands tried to keep a grip on the wheel. There was an explosion as the airbags deployed. I realized that I was completely flipping over at sixty mph and that I was helpless to stop it. My drinking and driving had finally caught up with me, I thought. I was certain that this was it; there was no way I could survive what was happening. In the last split second, I shut my eyes, ready to surrender my life there on that picturesque Oregon road.

I was forty-three years old and married, and three weeks earlier my father had died. The days I had spent in Milwaukee during his final hours and then the funeral had been so difficult that soon after my return to Oregon I went on a four-day crystal meth binge that very nearly destroyed my marriage. Maybe it would have ended then and there had my wife, Kristi, known that while she was out of town her husband was not only high, but running around Portland visiting adult bookstores, buying up women's clothing at the mall, visiting "jack shops" for dominatrix sessions, and spending hours at home in full makeup while calling phone sex lines and masturbating until his penis was raw and bleeding. My full-blown binge broke a streak of fourteen years without hard drugs, a dry period that began with my arrest in San Diego in the summer of 1983. I had survived four months in jail and met Kristi in 1986. The following year we moved to Oregon, where we fell in love with the forested land, a love that eventually drew us into the activist movement galvanized around protecting state forest from renewed logging.

We rented our first house in Mountaindale, a small town twenty miles west of Portland, and settled in with our cats Reba and Beefy. I was soon hired on at the Oregon Symphony, where my skills at innovative fund-raising produced new revenue and a secure position. Our wedding took place on our neighbors' property, whose acreage spread across a hidden valley among small hills covered in Douglas fir. On that special day, something happened to remind me of my long-held desire to become a woman as Kristi and I walked down a little dirt road toward the trout pond, where our guests had all gathered and a flute player was already in place. The sun had never shined bluer: it was that deep, early summer blue. The breeze was never more pleasant. And my bride looked resplendent in her secondhand wedding dress complemented with a garland of fresh flowers wrapped in a halo fashion around her head. Popeye, the sixteen-year-old German shepherd farm dog that lived on the property, followed behind us carrying a fireplace-size log in his mouth, a comical touch to our procession. Walking down the "aisle," I looked into Kristi's light blue eyes. I saw nothing but nurturing love emanating from them. Suddenly, however, a voice invaded this perfect moment, telling me I was playing a straight role for others instead of taking care of my true self.

"Think!" said this voice. "As much as you may want to be a male, you aren't, and this union is destined to end in failure."

It was a voice I knew all too well, one that had spoken to me my entire life, first asserting itself the day of my near drowning, when my parents told me to change out of the dress they had let me wear while my boy clothes dried. Now the voice told me, "You are a girl. It's *you* who should be in that wedding dress, marrying another woman. Don't do it. There's still time to change your mind and end this relationship. Find the courage to admit you were wrong and end this. Kristi will be better for it years from now, and you will too."

In San Diego, I hadn't been able to begin hormone therapy and the process of transitioning to female under medical supervision because I'd failed the drug test. And I never looked back, never revisited that option. And now I was about to take another step toward denying my inner self, ignoring what might be my last chance to live my life openly as the female I had known I was since that day at the lake. Perhaps, however, I could come clean to Kristi now before it was too late. Did I have the courage? As it turned out, I did not; right then the voice vanished and with it the courage to act. I told myself, all of that is in the past now, it's no longer who I am today. I'm in love with Kristi and I'm going to marry her! This interior pep talk brought me back from the brink, and as we approached the pond where the uplifting flute music played, applause broke out. I tingled from head to toe and felt a huge lump in my throat. After exchanging vows in front of family and friends, Kristi and I got into a small rowboat and paddled out to the middle of the pond. On cue, the guests opened sachets of trout pellet food that Kristi had spent much time putting together, tying each sachet with a pink or blue bow. The pellets arched through the air and all at once the water around our boat bubbled like a caldron as the trout thrashed about devouring the food. The flutist continued her playing, the guests were laughing, and I kissed my bride passionately, knowing this was the happiest day of my life.

There was a hard crash, the sound of glass breaking, screeching, and grinding as the truck came to a halt off the side of the lonely road. I opened my eyes to discover myself hanging sideways, held in by my seatbelt. The truck hadn't flipped but instead landed on the passenger side, which was completely crushed. Only one small space, where I was seated, remained untouched.

In the cracked rearview mirror I saw blood covering my arms and face. Realizing I must be bleeding badly someplace, I fought the urge to panic, struggling to keep from going into shock. With difficulty, I steadied my breathing. What if I was bleeding internally and had damaged organs? I began to shake violently as I studied the blood all over my arms, but a thought occurred to me—it was a very odd color for blood. It slowly dawned on me that it wasn't blood at all but blackberry juice! Earlier on my drive I had spotted a Himalayan blackberry bush, pulled over, and spent a good hour picking berries and sipping Green Death. I had a full bag of them next to me on the seat, and during the accident they had dumped over, flying everywhere.

Although it turned out I wasn't covered in blood, I now feared the truck would burst into flames at any moment, as the engine had died but was steaming and hissing noisily. I was determined to roll down my window and climb out. I undid the seat belt and boosted myself free and clear. It was like the Apollo moon landing as I climbed onto the top of my truck and surveyed the darkening night sky and the surrounding forest while a chill wind blew. I knew it would be awhile before a car came. Just before dropping down to the ground, I thought twice and went back into the cab to grab the empty bottle of Green Death, which somehow hadn't broken, as well as the pipe and weed. I then climbed out, scrambled to the ground, and tossed the pipe and weed into the ditch and hurled the bottle far into the trees. In doing so I noticed that my chest and arms hurt. Also, one leg was burned from the air bag explosion.

I saw headlights approaching. I knew whoever it was would stop once they saw my truck on its side. Sure enough, the car's driver pulled over. Out hopped a middle-aged man. Was I all right? he asked. Despite an aching soreness beginning to creep throughout my body, I said yes. He was an off-duty fireman and got right down to business, using his two-way car radio to call for law enforcement and setting out road flares to mark the accident scene. It took forty minutes for a Columbia County sheriff to arrive and take over. He asked if I had been drinking. I told him of course not, but he made me breathe into his face. I figured the jig was up; I'd be going down with my first-ever DUI. But, surprisingly, my breath didn't incriminate me. Then I realized I'd been saved by the blackberries. I'd been munching on them during the drive and my breath smelled only of wild berries.

The sheriff wasn't yet convinced. With a powerful flashlight, he scoured the entire area looking for any beer or liquor bottles, broken glass, anything that could tie me to alcohol. The foresight that had led me to toss everything into the forest had saved me from arrest. The sheriff asked again if I'd been drinking, and I very politely said no and that I would never, ever consider drinking and driving. I told him about the car coming the other way, forcing me to take evasive action to avoid a head-on collision. The flashlight actually revealed skid marks going the other direction, so there really might have been another car—maybe driven by another intoxicated driver.

After taking a detailed account of my story, the sheriff drove me home, a ride that took almost an hour. I was now hours overdue, and as soon as we pulled up the gravel road to my house, Kristi came flying out the front door. The look of sheer panic on her face made me momentarily forget how much my entire body ached and the excruciating burn on my leg. Still, I would not tell her what really happened, another deceit added to a long list. Kristi took me to the hospital where they checked me out for broken bones and dressed my burn. Fortunately, nothing was broken. They gave me pain pills and sent us on our way.

This accident scared me, and I vowed to quit drinking. This resolution was reinforced when I visited the junkyard to retrieve some personal items from my truck. I was shocked when I saw the brand-new Toyota in the daylight. It was completely smashed in with only that tiny bubble of space where I'd been seated left untouched. I was so lucky to be alive, I thought, staring at the wreck. I drove my rental car back to the scene of the accident for a closer look at those skid marks coming the other way. Yes, there they were all right. But could they have been made by a driver swerving to get out of *my* way? I had been very drunk and all of this could've been my fault. I glanced down into the road ditch and spotted something—my pipe and the film canister full of good bud that I had chucked frantically that evening. I scooped them up and lit up a bowl as I climbed back into my rental and headed home.

I enrolled in an eleven-week outpatient group counseling program. I did so kicking and screaming after learning at the orientation that I would have to quit smoking weed too. I argued that my problem was strictly with alcohol. But the therapists would have none of it; it was all or nothing. I reluctantly agreed to their terms.

Again, I hid this major step from Kristi, being too afraid to disclose how bad my drinking had gotten. The beginning was pure hell. I couldn't stop thinking about wanting a Green Death, wine, or a stiff Bombay gin and tonic. I wanted to smoke a joint so bad that in class I imagined myself rolling a fat one containing the best bud around, lighting it up, and handing it to the two therapists up front just to see the looks on their faces. Class ran from eight until noon, Tuesday through Friday. My employer at the time, the Oregon Symphony, was supportive of my sobriety and gave me paid time off to do this. I only had to chip in a nominal copay. Driving home after my workday was the toughest. I probably hadn't gone more than one or two days without drinking since my early twenties, so being sober was a total shock to my system. Before leaving downtown Portland, I would drive past the stores I knew stocked Green Death. (I had been in the habit of doing a round robin of these shops so each owner wouldn't know how often I actually drank the stuff.) I would park and sit in my truck staring at the store, savoring the malt liquor.

My normal routine prior to rehab had been to use mouthwash, eye drops, and aftershave just before pulling up the gravel road to the house so Kristi wouldn't know I'd been drinking or smoking. Once inside I'd say hello with the obligatory kiss, change out of my office clothes, go back outside and transfer the cooler I kept in the truck to the wood shed, where I had my third, sometimes fourth, bottle of Green Death, which I drank on ice out of a plastic glass that I kept out there. Kristi spent the evening hours lesson planning and preparing for our meetings at the Sierra Club, where we were co-chairs of the Tillamook State Forest Committee. I would prepare dinner, do the dishes, clean litter boxes, refill all the water and food dishes for our six cats and two dogs, sneaking outside here and there to drink and smoke for short periods of time. My guilt over this behavior was off the charts. The only reason I was doing all of this housework was so I could find opportunities to drink and smoke. Unbridled guilt over this was the reason Kristi received all the foot and body massages she did.

During rehab I was coming home sober for the first time in our twelve-year relationship and was at a loss as to how to interact. Without the Green Death and weed to numb me, I had to try harder than ever before to talk with my wife. It was when I was in this already very fragile state that a crisis hit. I was barely two weeks into group therapy when I realized Kristi and I were leaving on a weeklong camping trip that had been planned for months. It was our summer vacation, and we were to drive up to British Columbia. I was not mentally prepared for this but, nonetheless, after arguing with my two therapists, I got the green light to go. One therapist virtually accused me of using this trip as an excuse to jettison group therapy and go drink. She was right, which in the end was my salvation, because I was determined to prove her wrong.

Every day during the trip I struggled and could only think about wanting what I could no longer have. Several times I almost caved when we entered a grocery store. All of that cold Canadian beer looked so refreshing to me. Not until the third night did Kristi ask where my usual three coolers of beer and wine were. This was the moment I'd been waiting for and it all came gushing out, as I wanted her to become part of the effort, part of the team, to help rid myself of this addiction. I told her my drinking and smoking had gotten out of hand and that I had recently enrolled in alcohol/drug addiction group therapy. I told her I wanted her to be my best friend and help me with this. I wanted her to hold me, hug me, kiss me, tell me it was going to be all right. Deep down, I wanted the guilt to go away. I wanted to reconnect with my wife, to rebuild the relationship we'd had earlier in our marriage. I wanted us to be the A-team again, as we used to call ourselves.

Instead of love in return, there was anger. She was angry that I hadn't told her about the group therapy earlier, notwithstanding my explanation that I'd withheld the information over fear of failure. The rest of our trip was tarred by mutual silent resentment and anger. The dark mood continued after we returned home. I started to resent all the chores, the massages, everything I was giving her, without getting anything back. I casually mentioned that it was out of guilt that I did those massages: "Guilt over my drinking and smoking behind your back." I was coming clean, trying to open new lines of communication, but my confessions only made her angrier. Now for the first time in our marriage, I was beginning to realize that it might not last. All that numbing I had done had created a dynamic that was now very entrenched and difficult to alter. One day she declared that she was there to support me in my effort to quit drinking. Her words were lackluster and without conviction. I felt devastated and cried quietly later in private. How ironic this had become. The major reason I wanted to quit drinking and smoking was to reconnect with my wife, and now I felt her slipping away little by little.

Yet I made it through the eleven weeks. The night of my graduation I drove my old route home, going by the little stores that stocked bottles of Green Death. But now I had the tools to fend off urges and not sink into negative ritualistic behavior patterns. I had the weapons, strength, desire, and ability to beat the addiction. I talked with Kristi about my graduation but sensed there just wasn't anything sincere in her response. I could feel the life being drained out of our relationship and felt helpless to stop it. I was out of ideas. I even tried to open up a sexual intimacy discussion, suggesting maybe we could set aside a time for that and be more adventuresome. All she could say in reply was, "No kinky stuff."

I was devastated. My faith in our troubled marriage was shrinking. Denise's time was drawing closer.

Part 3

1983–1997

*B*reakfast came very early my first morning at the Metropolitan Correctional Center. I managed to ask the inmate guarding me for the time. "Five a.m." he answered. How could I possibly eat breakfast at that hour? I barely touched my food but did drink the coffee, and soon my tray was taken away. I expected that very soon I'd be taken out and at least be allowed to walk around the room a little. There were six psychiatric cells in a row inside a bigger room that had another security door, and there was a shower that also had a security door. The other inmates locked up with me in their own cells were all let out one at a time for an hour to wander about in the bigger room. I wasn't. My tiny cell became a nightmare; I was experiencing withdrawal symptoms from crank and Quaaludes and the isolation, while safer than the general population, took a greater toll than I had anticipated. I was frightened, and I didn't know what was going to happen to me next. But in this place, of course, none of that mattered.

That night—I could tell it was night because things became quieter out in the main ward area—the guy in the cell next to mine started acting crazy: screaming at the top of his lungs, yelling obscenities, telling Jesus to come and get him, the works. This went on for hours and I couldn't sleep. Finally, I heard the outer door unlock and I got down onto the floor to peek through the trap door where our food was slipped through. Looking out that narrow opening, I could see as three guys in white coats came in, one of them wielding a large syringe full of something, the other two carrying leather restraints. They went into the guy's cell and I heard him being strapped down to his bed, as he sang "Camptown Races"—*Goin' to run all night, Goin' to run all day, Bet my money on the bob-tailed nag, Somebody bet on the bay*—with its *doo-dah, doo-dah* refrain. Then it was quiet for a minute as they injected him. I thought, why not do the same? I'd love an injection to knock me out. But the drug didn't knock him out totally; he started muttering to himself nonstop. An inmate screamed, "Shut the fuck up!" which brought back the team of white coats for another shot. This time it worked; there was silence. The suicide-watch orderly came to my trap door and handed me a rolled tobacco cigarette, lit it for me, and went back to his post. This was the first act of kindness I experienced inside the MCC.

For the next five days I was kept in that cell, my world limited to what little I could see through the window slit on my door. On the fifth day I had a visitor: Ed, who had decided to serve as my attorney. I was very surprised to see him. I bombarded him with questions about the "outside world," as I had begun calling it. He did his best to answer, telling me that soon I'd have another court date at which a federal judge would be assigned to my case and I would enter a plea. That was when, he said, he would no longer be able to serve as my attorney on this case. I would have to ask for a public defender at my next court appearance, and he would be there to officially withdraw so that it wouldn't be a problem for me to secure legal representation. It wasn't about being paid, he explained. My case was just too big, there were conflicts of interest, and it was beyond his capabilities. I repeatedly asked what he thought was going to happen to me, but he said it was too early to tell, and when he got up to leave, I clung to him like a frightened kitten to keep him there so we could just keep talking. After he was gone I lay back down on my hard bed, buried my head in the tiny pillow, and began to sob uncontrollably. Moments later I looked down and saw another rolled cigarette with a book of matches appear through the trap door.

My dreams became vivid; I was free, flying away, soaring above the world and finding the exhilaration of being out of my cell simply wondrous. Then I would wake up, roused by the sounds in the main area as breakfast was being prepared. My thoughts would crystallize and I'd stare up at the dreary ceiling, wanting my dream back. One morning the guys in white coats came for my neighbor. They strapped him onto a gurney and wheeled him out. I only found out later that he was in for robbing a bank— using his finger as a gun. Near the end of my first week a psychiatrist visited me, a woman I felt comfortable talking to as she seemed kind and genuine. I begged her to let me out into the adjacent ward room. I needed to stand, walk around, look out the window at the outside world. She allowed this, and once I was in the other room, I started sobbing. I realized what a mess I looked like with my permed girly hair and no shower in six days. She asked if I'd ever been committed to a state hospital. This question put me on guard, making me suspicious that I was being set up to be shuttled off and incarcerated at a state mental institution, but I answered truthfully that I had not. She left me in that room with the outer security door locked. I looked indirectly into the other cells for glimpses of the crazies. But none looked as frightful as me. At a large window I peered through slits between the cement blocks; people walked to and fro. I felt an intense jealousy at their freedom to do whatever they wanted. How was I going to survive, how would I get through this? I understood I was only at the beginning of this ordeal and would have to figure out how to navigate the long road ahead.

The head psychiatrist of all the federal prisons in Southern California came to have a chat with me. He said it was obvious that I was no longer suicidal and would have to be transferred to another floor, as this one was strictly for inmates with medical needs. I asked if this meant placing me in the general population and he said yes. As all my fears rushed back. I protested, saying I stood a good chance of being preyed on, telling him about the tattoos on my behind and what they said. When he didn't seem to understand or believe me, I offered to show him. I jumped up and lowered my pants. There was a momentary silence before he furrowed his brow and said, "We'll go ahead and keep you on this floor."

That floor, the fifth, was nicknamed the Mexican Country Club because of the many illegal immigrants from dirt-poor areas of Latin America who were incarcerated there as they awaited disposition of their cases. The inmates on the fifth floor were the trusted ones, comprising only a handful within the jail. Our duties included suicide watch, helping with inmate exams, handing food to inmates confined to the tuberculosis unit, and rigorous cleaning to keep the entire floor in tip-top condition. Unlike the other floors, which were overcrowded and loud, ours had carpeting, a large television, a pool table, and most important of all, privacy. I knew I needed to stay in the Mexican Country Club permanently, and so when an inmate named Lupe noticed how I mostly just lounged around and smoked cigarettes all day whenever I was out of my cell, he recommended I help out, since doing so would improve my chances of remaining there. I thought of the alternative and at once "volunteered" for the cleaning crew, sometimes working ten hours a day. I thought miserably about how my life had changed as I cleaned toilet bowls, scrubbed and waxed floors, and awaited a prison term. One time I was placed inside the pharmacy to clean the shelves; I knew this meant they really trusted me, since there were plenty of good drugs in there. And while it would've been easy to steal a handful of pills and get high, I couldn't stand the idea of being high and in prison.

Two female guards, both on the night shift, sort of liked me. One was deeply religious and always talked to me about Jesus Christ. She and Lupe were tight because they were both Christians, but I suspected there was more to their bond than Jesus. Unlike the inmates on the other floors, I no longer had regular lockdown hours, which was how I came to notice this guard going in and out of Lupe's cell. She would tell me they had been in deep discussion about Jesus Christ, the Lord. I played along. Soon she was lingering outside my cell before locking it late at night. It occurred to me that if I wanted, she could make my night very interesting.

I shot a lot of pool with the male guards to try and connect with them. I recall a guard once asking me what I was going to do if I got hard time. I looked at him and said, "Deal with it." He had seen my tattoos during strip searches, and I knew he was trying to really frighten me with a question like that. He took me for a softie. But I was clever, and I had increasing fortitude and a deep resolve to get myself out of this mess, none of which he could begin to fathom. He underestimated me, which was the way I liked it. My whole life I have always been underestimated. This can be a great advantage, especially when those against you are wrong. I was in a high-stakes poker game inside the MCC and was determined to walk away from the table the winner. An inner strength grew inside me. Without drugs or alcohol, my thinking had become clear and direct. Being busted, I began to realize, might have even saved me from an early death. There was goodness in everything; I felt very alive for the first time in many years. What a peaceful, wonderful feeling to have considering where I was.

I eventually called my parents. It was a very sad conversation. I explained that I could get out if I posted bail; my father turned me down flat. He would have to put the house up for collateral. "Too risky," he said, for he feared that the government would somehow take it. I think he was more worried about me disappearing. And he might have been right. It had crossed my mind to flee to Mexico were I to post bail. He went on to say that when my trial came he would fly out to San Diego, and that no matter what happened I was still a young man and once released I would be able to rebuild my life. I could tell I was being kissed off by him, and I almost lost my temper. Instead, I said glibly, "I understand and hope you and Mom have a great rest of the weekend," then hung up, vowing never to call them again for anything.

A rather amazing thing happened at the Mexican Country Club. I was in the linen room one morning grabbing the fresh sheets needed for changing bedding in the psych ward. In between the linens, I came across a prison dress. It had to be there by accident; I didn't even know there were such things like this in prison, yet here it was. The dress was one piece, beige in color, and the material was somewhat coarse. But it sure looked liked it would fit me and so I immediately took it back to my cell to hide. That evening as soon as I had the chance, I put it on. Even without a mirror, I knew it fit me really well. For the first time since my arrest I felt a surge of femininity spread through me. I lay down on my bed and fell asleep in that dress, reassured that in my isolated wing, no one would come around to bother me. In the morning I smiled when I realized I was still in the dress. I put it away for later and was so thrilled I had this little piece of the outside world for myself.

*V*ince visited for the first time, lifting my spirits immeasurably and making me laugh. Even more important, he delivered a wise message. I needed to start thinking about myself, he said, "because no one else is going to." He elaborated by asking me who on the outside had offered me anything, who had come to tell me not to worry, who had offered to pay bail, who had hired an attorney on my behalf? And how, he asked, did I feel about Tom, my codefendant, having his case severed from mine and getting out on bail and hiring a top-gun defense attorney? After three months of incarceration, who had offered me anything? he asked. These were tough questions I had been avoiding because I didn't want to go there. In our conversation, Vince stressed that no one was going to free me except me. He was absolutely right. Neither Tom nor my own public defender cared about my circumstances. That day I began to formulate a plan to approach the cops. Vince put me in touch with someone named Ben, who happened to be a client of his.

Ben came to meet with me. I found him to be bright and articulate and an effective communicator. "Why are you doing this?" I asked. "What do you get out of this?"

That's when I found out that he had been busted not too long ago with ten kilos of cocaine. He'd been dealing for about three years when the NTF caught up with him, and down he went. If he could get me to cooperate, it could help lessen his sentence, which hadn't been handed down yet. Like me, he was striving to avoid a long prison term.

Ben told me that I was being played by Lewis Wenzell, Tom's attorney, and by my public defender. It turned out she was a good friend of Wenzell's. "That's why your case was severed from Tom's." It was a common practice to isolate one of the defendants in drug cases so that the one left in jail, feeling powerless, would take the biggest rap. He told me that in order to get out, I would have to agree to be available as a possible witness for the prosecution should my former codefendant choose to go to trial. I would also have to agree to work with the NTF on at least one case, becoming a confidential informant, or CI, to help develop a case and bring down another dealer, someone with whom I'd had contact before I was busted. Cooperating in this matter would weigh greatly in my eventual sentencing and even lead to a recommendation of probation instead of a jail term. Ever since Vince's visit I had been trying to digest the idea of betraying Tom. It wasn't in my blood to behave that way. What changed my attitude was the fresh understanding that prison had imparted a lesson, which was to never forget where you come from. I had dropped deep into the world of addiction, drug dealing, and false friends. I was much stronger than any of that but had lost my way. Also tipping the balance was the ongoing contentious manner of my public defender, who had turned venomous when I first brought up the subject of cooperating.

"I'm in," I told Ben and returned to my cell in a daze. Everything seemed to be happening so fast. It was a blur. I could sense the outside gushing in like a pool filling rapidly with water; for the first time in months I began to think about the outside and living there again. But not with glee and joy—like the drowning man I was, I was panicking. How could I survive? I'd be leaving the safety of the club, where I didn't have to think about anything. Then it hit me how institutionalized I must have become if I was viewing jail as a place of safety.

The next morning I awoke to find I had a terrible herpes outbreak all over my chin. My stressful state intensified when I met my public defender in the afternoon. I told her about my decision, and she implored me to reconsider, saying I was getting in way over my head and questioning my trust of the NTF after the way I had been set up and busted. She claimed it was a network shot through with corruption and that when they were through with me, I'd be tossed aside "like a piece of used toilet paper." Her words were so strong that I almost reconsidered, until I thought of Vince, the one person I knew and trusted. He would not steer me wrong on this. His word was gold to me, and in the end that was how I made my final decision. Two days later I had a new attorney, Michael Sideman.

I awoke the day before Thanksgiving with a strong hunch I would be released that same day. I started having doubts about my intuition when, at around three, a guard told me I was heading down to intake for a meeting. I was escorted to the first floor. There before me stood Brian, whom I hadn't seen since the night I got busted. We headed over to a room in the courthouse across the street where I met with representatives from the NTF and the DEA. I signed papers agreeing to be a confidential informant for the NTF. I also met Charlie, the man I'd be reporting to and working with. While he seemed friendly, I couldn't help but feel very nervous at the prospect of working with cops, my sworn enemy going back to childhood. Cops had never treated me with anything but disrespect.

"We're getting you out this evening," Charlie announced. Hearing this promise made me giddy. I was going to be free! No more being locked in a cell, no more prison nights, no more prison food, no more inmates to deal with, no more guards to deal with, no more strip searches, no more handcuffs, no more lockdowns. *I was going to be free.*

An hour after being escorted back to my cell, an older guard from intake who occasionally worked on my floor showed up with a kindly smile on his face. "Let's go," he told me. "You're being released." On the way down to intake, which was now outtake in reverse, this guard ventured a few comments about my survival there. "You probably don't remember, but I was the one who escorted you up to the fifth floor your first night. You were a real mess, and I thought there was no way you'd make it in here, that you were heading for a commitment in a state hospital." He never wanted to see me in here again. "Turn your life around," he counseled. "You're very smart and clever. Make something of yourself."

The elevator door opened; he walked me over to the release area and disappeared.

My street clothes, wallet, and keys were returned to me. A very attractive blonde guard handed me my clothes with a knowing look and a smile. Clearly, she knew my underclothes were a hot matching bra and panty set. In a private area I lovingly put them on, feeling once again the wonderfulness of lingerie on my body. I dropped my prison clothes in the hamper, including the prison dress, which I had brought down from my cell in a paper bag. Maybe after it was laundered, I thought, it would end up back in the linen closet for someone else like me to find. A different guard escorted me to the front entrance. Then it happened. The glass doors parted, and I stepped out into the dark San Diego night. I was only wearing the lightweight short sleeve shirt that I had on that hot August night of the bust, which seemed like eons ago. Now it was chilly out. As I stood near the entrance, something caught my attention. It was a growing light, quite bright. I leaned back, scanning the many stories of the MCC, which appeared as a great monolith. There, just cresting over the top of the building, a full moon appeared, flooding me in light. I remained bent backward for a long moment, awestruck by the celestial show, a force of good, akin to a goddess high in the sky welcoming me back to freedom.

The night of my release I had $750, the cash that had been in my wallet. But I had no home, no car, no friends, no place to go. I got rip-roaring drunk and ended up at Ed's in the middle of the night. The late hour and drinking must've seemed excusable given the circumstances, since Ed didn't turn me away. He even had good news for me the next day. A former customer, he said, was holding $3,000 for me. I couldn't believe what I was hearing. This meant I'd have something to get started on: money to buy a used car, get a studio apartment and look for a regular job—I had no intention of ever again dealing drugs, nor would I ever take crank or any other drug again. Only alcohol and pot from here on out, I vowed. Ed grilled steak that evening, and during the celebratory dinner he pulled me aside, saying he had something to show me in his garage. We went in and after flicking on the light, he abruptly left me alone. I saw why. There sat boxes full of my women's clothes, wigs, makeup, magazines, sex toys. All of it was there, even my 1968 bottle of Château Lafite Rothschild. I had wondered what happened to my belongings after that horrible night and now I knew. Ed had gone over to my apartment and cleaned things up for me. He did it out of friendship. I was very touched by his act of kindness.

Soon after, I bought a used car, a 1967 Dodge Dart, and found a studio apartment. I got further on my feet by scoring a job with a company that employed local tour guides. But an even bigger coup came after I auditioned for a part in the chorus of the San Diego Gilbert and Sullivan Repertoire Theatre Company production of *The Sorcerer*. I had done theater in high school and taken acting classes at SDSU, and when I got selected for the chorus I was thrilled beyond belief. This company was the real deal: You had to know your part, the music, lyrics, stage blocking . . . everything. Gary Owens, the director, was demanding, professional, and had high expectations of his cast. I was part of a truly professional production.

Meanwhile, the NTF team wanted me to begin approaching my past business contacts to see if any of them wanted to work with me. I knew the drill, since it was the exact thing that had ensnared me. I racked my brains to think of someone out there who might not know what had happened to me. I settled on Rick, who owed me thousands of dollars. If he was surprised to see me the evening I appeared at his door, he didn't show it. I was nervous, wondering if he had any inkling of my whereabouts these past months, and I worried he'd figure out that I was "wired" for this visit. I'd been coached to turn the discussion to a cocaine buy—the bigger the better. So after some small talk I asked him if he had the money he owed me. As I expected, the answer was no. Now I felt less guilty about "doing" him and proceeded to turn the talk to buying cocaine from him.

I was infuriated at how readily he said he could get his hands on as much cocaine as I needed, just moments after claiming he didn't have a dime of the money owed me. I talked about getting five kilos and then matter-of-factly explained there was another person involved he would have to meet because this individual controlled the money and the deal. We both stood to make quite a bit of money, I said, and after crunching some numbers, Rick concurred. Again, there was no mention of payback of his debt. Later at the NTF van parked nearby, Charlie told me I did great and said my next move would be to introduce him to Rick to do a controlled buy of an eighth of cocaine, the "hook" that would give the NTF probable cause to start monitoring him.

That subsequent meeting went smoothly, mirroring the initial one Al had set up for me with Brian a year ago. As Rick casually pulled out an eight ball and slid it across the table under his hand to Charlie, the money went the other way—three crisp $100 bills, for sure marked, just as mine had been. Later, Charlie told me the cocaine was good quality and now we needed to put pressure on Rick to tell us just how much cocaine he could pull together. The NTF wanted a big haul. They were all about busting someone and then seeing if that person would "turn" and finger the higher-ups who had provided the cocaine.

By the time of the bust, Rick had completely dumped me and was working exclusively with Charlie. If he only knew what I knew, I thought, and how his sneaky underhandedness had just made my job that much easier. Things soon came to a crescendo. A little less than a week after the hook, Charlie called to tell me the deal had happened but with a bit of a surprise ending for the

Feds: Rick had only four ounces of cocaine with him at his house. Charlie had told him it wasn't enough and the deal was off. Rick had reacted by scooping up the four ounces and leaving out the front door, only to discover two NTF team members casing the front yard. He ran off into the darkness and before being tackled managed to toss two ounces into the bushes and the other two onto a condo balcony. The NTF recovered the cocaine from the balcony, and in a house search they found twenty-five pounds of low-grade pot, which was included in the evidence. It wasn't the haul they had wanted, but I had made an honest effort.

$\mathcal{M}$y life since jail was enjoying a complete renaissance, despite a pattern of excessive drinking. After the Gilbert and Sullivan production ended, I auditioned for *The Martian Chronicles*, by Ray Bradbury. The director was "Doc" Adams, a former professor of mine at SDSU. I saw my chances as being slim to none with so many good actors at the audition and a cast of just twelve. When I got the call from the assistant director letting me know I had been cast, I was so overwhelmed I could barely thank her.

Meanwhile, the NTF contacted me again to try and snag one more person. I came up with a guy Al had once hooked me up with for MDA, a recreational party drug that is the precursor the MDMA or ecstasy. While similar, it's a more hard-core stimulant and psychedelic. Charlie let me handle the controlled buy on my own this time, and in my meeting with the dealer he wholeheartedly agreed to meet my friend. After leaving him and walking to my car I found myself burning with temptation to pinch some of the MDA now in my bag. The NTF's listening van was parked several blocks away, well out of sight, plus they weren't searching me anymore. I had the MDA packet out of my pocket when I suddenly stopped. I just couldn't go back to that kind of life. I knew that if I did some, I'd be back on the road to serious addiction. I slid the packet back into my pocket, got into my car, and drove away.

Several days later I received an excited call from Charlie. The lab that had analyzed the MDA reported that it was over 90 percent pure. Having something this pure come along was rare, and now he was very eager to move ahead. I made the arrangements for the pair to meet in a few days. We did it the same way as the last time around, having the meeting at a restaurant, during which Charlie pushed really hard for a large quantity of the MDA. I was glad when the negotiations were over and I could step out of that crowded, noisy place into the fresh evening air. I told Charlie my thoughts on how things went, which was that he might have scared the guy off. Charlie said it wouldn't have been the first time and then gave me some fantastic news. From here on out I wouldn't have to do anything more except testify at Tom's trial, if there was one. The NTF, he explained, was letting me go; my days as a CI had come to an end. I certainly wasn't about to question the decision. I shook Charlie's hand and said goodbye. He had been both my captor and liberator. In a strange way, I would miss him.

The rehearsal schedule for *The Martian Chronicles* was grueling and went on right up to the date that had been set for the cast to leave for the ornate Norris Theatre in Palos Verdes, a coastal enclave of Los Angeles. There we rehearsed even more (until several hours before the curtain went up). Even as we were rehearsing for the final time, Doc Adams was reworking the script and blocking. I was very pleased with the revised script, because Doc had given me more lines and stage presence. These changes, coming from the master, as I thought of him, were the surest sign I could want that he liked my work. Our three-day run at the Norris was fantastic. All four performances sold out, and as a cast we fully hit our stride, leading the audience to frenzied appreciation, as evidenced by the standing ovations. Finally, after all the revisions and endless rehearsals, Doc Adams was satisfied. At the cast party, he glowed with praise. After the show closed, and I had received another

$150 stipend for months of work, I kept hoping the phone would ring and someone on the other end would tell me the production had sold and we were off on a national tour. That never happened. I wanted to continue in acting, but not making any money at it was beginning to get old.

I got word from the United States district attorney telling me I needed to testify in the coming week at Tom's drug trial. The assistant U.S. district attorney, Alberto A. Arevalo, was young, bright, and articulate, and he wanted a conviction. In our first interview he asked about my huge phone bills, presumably thinking that I might be a bigger dealer than my plea bargain suggested. Looking him straight in the eye, I told him all those calls were to sex lines and that I had been a crank addict and also addicted to calling dominatrixes, spending hours on the phone with them. "There's more," I said, "much more we need to talk about before I take the stand." He gently stopped me, smiled warmly, and re-assuringly said he understood. Moments later, Ben strolled into the office. Was I ever happy to see him; now I knew we had something going. I opened up to both of them about my private life. I told them it was a certainty that the defense team knew about my cross-dressing and would try to rattle me with it. They listened to my tale, which I condensed into a crisp five-minute account. After I was finished, Alberto said that no matter what, I had to tell the truth on the stand.

The morning of the trial, I walked into the federal building and proceeded directly up to Alberto's office. When the door opened, I was shocked to see Al sitting there. I felt anger rise up in me and I walked straight over to him, ignoring Alberto's cautionary warnings to calm down. I had one word to say to him. "Why?" I asked with a menacing glare, wanting to pummel him into the ground. Rarely had I ever felt so much anger toward a human being as I did in that moment. He sheepishly fed me a line about how he did it for love of America, that the drug situation in this country had gotten out of hand. He said he was "surprised" to hear how long I was locked up. I left him and the office to cool off, not believing one word he'd said. Later I would learn from Alberto that Al had in fact been a paid confidential informant. He needed money desperately and had decided the easiest way to get it was to contact the DEA.

For the trial's opening day, Tom's defense lawyer, Lewis Wenzell, had come up with a trick, namely, packing the chambers with law students bussed in from the University of San Diego. He wanted to put on a show, create a spectacle, by agitating and embarrassing me in front of a large audience. It worked, too, because when I entered the courtroom and saw the crowd, I was greatly upset. As it turned out, Alberto knew in advance about the charade and just as soon as Wenzell rose to deliver his opening statement, Alberto got up and asked to approach the bench. He spoke quietly with Federal Court Judge Gordon Thompson for a few moments and immediately following the discussion, Thompson sounded his gavel and announced that court was adjourned for the day. As I walked past Wenzell, I matched the devilish look he had directed at me just minutes earlier.

When the trial resumed several days later, the courtroom was practically empty. Our delaying tactic had worked; the law students were gone. Now, though, it was time for me to testify, and there was one guy in the chamber's audience who wouldn't take his eyes off me, glaring with hatred. Probably a private investigator for the defense team, I thought. The first part of my testimony was easy. I was calmly questioned by Alberto and encouraged to tell my story of the events as they unfolded that night almost a year ago. I was steady and direct in my narrative, looking at both him and Judge Thompson.

When Wenzell stood up to question me, I immediately sensed he was overconfident and had underestimated me and my ability to communicate. His first line of attack was to ask what I did for a living. "You're an actor, right? And actors can make people believe anything, right?" I calmly informed him that I worked as a freelance tour guide and that acting was merely my hobby, adding that as an actor I'd made a grand total of $300 in stipends.

He went into great detail on the seized evidence that was found that night before asking me if I recognized any of it sitting in sealed plastic bags on the evidence table. I sought permission from the judge to leave the witness stand to get a closer look at the evidence, not to stall but to help ease my tension, which he granted. I took my time in getting up and walking over to the table. I already knew that everything on that table came from my house. Nevertheless, I leisurely looked at my old weighing scales, the processing screens, baking dishes, mortar and pestle, and sealed ounces of cocaine. When Lewis Wenzell asked me again about the items, I admitted they were all mine, except for the cocaine, because I didn't own any of it at the time of my arrest that evening. That was not the answer he wanted, and I was delighted the jury got that last part loud and clear—a qualifying statement that just popped into my head at the last second. Shortly after this line of questioning Wenzell came back at me with the accusation I was expecting, which he threw out with a cold brusqueness: "Do you wear women's clothes and go by the name of Denise?"

I was about to answer yes when I was cut off by USDA Alberto Arevalo, who objected. Judge Thompson sustained the objection and did so again when Wenzell tried the stunt a second time by asking me if I liked to wear dresses. Judge Thompson reproved Wenzell, saying he would not tolerate any more of this line of questioning to the witness. Observing the jury, I could tell that they were put off by the defense attorney's attack. It made him look like he was not in touch with his client or the case, while making me appear as a victim. I wasn't surprised when right after this bungled tactic I was abruptly dismissed. Although I wanted badly to remain in the courtroom and listen to the forthcoming testimony by Al, I had agreed to return to the office upstairs. On my way out I glanced over at the guy still staring at me, full of hate, and gave him a nice wide smile. "Closet case" was all I could think as I made my exit. I don't know what it was, he just gave off a self-loathing vibe.

In the lobby I ran into Brian, who told me I'd done a great job on the stand. The NTF was grateful, he said, and would put a good word in with the USDA office about the work I'd done for them. He offered me a ride home, and as we left the building, I spotted Tom, not more than twenty-five yards away, surrounded by his friends—my former ones—who had been too cowardly to show their faces inside the courtroom. They saw me too and glared. Brian then made a brilliant call by telling me that even if I didn't need a ride, I should hop in the front seat anyway. "It'll look good," he said. We got into a San Diego sheriff's car and drove past Tom and his entourage. I lowered the car window and smiled at all of them.

$\mathcal{M}$y new attorney, Michael Sideman, called a few days later. Would I be willing, he asked, to plead guilty in federal court to using a communication device, namely the telephone, to facilitate a drug transaction? All other charges were to be dropped and there would be no mention of cocaine in the conviction. I readily agreed to this and a few weeks later found myself back in federal court, this time to plead out and be sentenced. The morning of my court date I had my final meeting with Alberto. He said his office and the NTF had done everything they could in the presentencing report to ensure that my sentence was mild. This did not raise my comfort level one bit because I knew "Five and Dime" Thompson had a reputation as the strictest judge on the bench for drug offenses. When I came into the almost empty courtroom, I was very surprised to see all my supporters present: Charlie, Ben, Brian, Vince, and the district attorney were all in my corner that day.

Sideman opened things by submitting my guilty plea. Alberto said the government had no objections to my guilty plea, dropped all other charges, and noted that my cooperation with his office had been instrumental in securing the conviction of my former codefendant, now in state custody awaiting sentencing. Then the district attorney went further and stated for the record that he recommended that the presentencing guidelines be followed, with me being placed on probation.

I was asked a series of routine questions by Judge Thompson before being given the opportunity to make a statement. I rose and looked about the courtroom. I had planned to just say thank you and sit back down again, but instead I launched into a spontaneous soliloquy about how I felt so much better today as a person compared to the way I did the night I was arrested, how I'd learned my lesson and only wanted to improve my life from here on out. Then I thanked everyone present and sat down. There was a short adjournment before court resumed and I was instructed to stand.

Judge Thompson sentenced me to five years in prison—I froze in terror. But next he uttered the word *suspended*, meaning no prison time as long as I stayed out of trouble. He said he saw no reason not to go along with the district attorney's recommended sentence and gave me a five-year federal probation term. Finally, looking at me, he wished me luck, saying, "I never want to see your face ever again in his courtroom, because if I do, I'll come down hard." With that, it was all over. "Your little speech at the end may have kept you out of prison," Charlie told me afterward. "You impressed the judge with that. Nice work." I wasn't acting, but it couldn't have hurt that I did act and was comfortable expressing myself on my feet. For once, me and my big mouth got me *out* of trouble.

I was back in group therapy with Vince and six other men who were into cross-dressing. As a transsexual, rather than a transvestite,

I never quite felt comfortable with them. Their motivations were different than mine, and several had beards and dressed without looking very feminine. There was a very male vibe, in other words, and even though I wasn't dressing at the moment, none of the urges of wanting to be a woman had gone away. I was repressing my inner self, dulling it with booze and pot. I knew it was only a matter of time before things exploded again. There was no escaping who I really was.

Group therapy helped in one way: it was good to hear other people's stories and to learn about their struggles. One member had a wife who showed compassion toward him and accommodated his need to dress up; she was kind of the top in their relationship. I met her at a social held one weekend. She was gorgeous and came to the party with a riding crop. I was jealous but had my fun that night too. I had invited Sheila and got dressed beforehand at her house. This marked the first time in my life that I went out dressed without being high on crank. What a revelation. I actually looked stunning when not sweating profusely from drugs. At the party, Sheila noticed my longings, and back at her place she eventually had me spread-eagle over her coffee table, skirt up, panties down. She penetrated me with one of her dildos while stoking me to a satisfying climax. Then I worshipped her loins and she smeared my makeup all over my face as she climaxed. It was little trysts like these that kept me going and learning how to feel comfortable being who I was without drugs. This was a period of growth for me, but sadly I soon lost Sheila to a boyfriend. I felt abandoned and couldn't help wondering if she'd left me because I was so strange. Once again I retreated from society: I quit group therapy and pretended my inner self didn't exist, using alcohol to numb my despair.

I got cast again by the Gilbert and Sullivan Company, this time for *H.M.S. Pinafore*. I now had some solo parts, a step up. But two weeks into the schedule I got a call that changed everything. An incentive house—a company that provides incentive programs to businesses, who then offer them to their employees as rewards—based in New Orleans and connected to domestic and international corporate travel, called out of the blue after hearing about me. Would I be interested in working on a large corporate group coming to New Orleans? My airfare, lodging, and meals would be covered by the company. As fantastic as the offer sounded, the dates conflicted with the theater production. I stalled as long as possible but in the end the money and the lure of potential international travel were too strong and I withdrew from the cast of *H.M.S. Pinafore.* It was not an easy decision; I actually cried, anxious over whether or not I'd made the right choice. I hadn't. Three days after quitting the cast, the incentive house called back telling me the group had canceled. I'd thrown my place away for nothing. In desperation I contacted Gilbert and Sullivan. Naturally, my spot had already been recast. My theater work ended right there; I never got onstage again. Yet new opportunities were soon to surface to not only work in international travel but to live abroad and start my own successful travel tour company. That chapter of my life unfolded in Costa Rica not long after meeting Kristi, the person who became the love of my life for many years.

I met Kristi after shifting from tour guide work to telemarketing, which I found I had a knack for. I was selling subscriptions at the Old Globe Theater, a San Diego institution, when one day I heard the voice of a new hire on the other side of the phone room. At first I didn't pay much attention to her, but I did notice that she was good on the phone, except for one important thing. When it came time to close on a subscription order, she just didn't have it in her to ask for a credit card, depending more on the trust of the potential new subscriber to mail in a check, which was always risky, since often the person would change their mind and not do it. Getting a credit card number locked in not only the order but your commission, too.

It was a Friday, a payday, and I had money in my wallet. Kristi walked past me and stopped nearby to chat with our supervisor. I suddenly realized I was attracted to her. That day she was wearing tight jeans with a pretty belt and top. With her cute curly blonde hair, she reminded me of an older version of Shirley Temple. Toward the end of our shift I approached her and asked if she would like to go out for some sushi and sake. "Sushi? . . . Sake?" She had no idea what I was talking about, which made her even more endearing. I explained that sushi was Japanese food and that sake was a rice wine, heated up, that went down very smoothly. She accepted. At my favorite sushi restaurant in Hillcrest, we grabbed seats at the sushi bar right in front of the chef, and the first thing I ordered was a large bottle of warm sake.

I never thought anyone could fall in love after just one date, but I did that night. I kept looking into her dancing eyes, at her smiling face, pearl white teeth, and hair that tossed about. She made me laugh when, after a few tiny cups of sake, she told me how she was feeling buzzed and that she liked sake. She mastered sushi eating right away, taking the chopsticks to grab a piece, dunk it in the soy sauce, then add some ginger and wasabi before popping it all in her mouth. She had a charming, positive outlook; her freshness bowled me over. I walked back to my car in a daze, stunned at how fast I'd fallen for this woman. This had never happened to me, and when I arrived at a poker game organized by a couple of friends later that night, I couldn't stop thinking about her.

This magical night ended on a sour note, though not in any way related to Kristi. I was then living in a largely female communal household that had a strict policy about drinking and pot smoking. When I arrived back there very early in the morning, I thought I would quietly slip unobserved into my bedroom. To my surprise, one my housemates was in the kitchen, packing a lunch for a Sierra Club hike she was going on. It was impossible to hide how drunk and stoned I was, and I slinked off to my room under her glare, knowing my days at this house were most likely at an end. Sure enough, at the next weekly house meeting I was given a two-month notice to find a new place. Alone in my room, I cried despondently. I had squandered a great living situation all because I couldn't stop drinking and smoking. These behaviors were ingrained in me, and I felt utterly powerless to do anything to stop.

I saw Kristi often, frequently going up to Del Mar, where she lived. Our first sexual encounter occurred outside, near her house in a grove of Torrey pine trees, a rare native species with local iconic status. It was getting dark and we tussled around on the ground, and then she let me go down on her. That same night I slept over for the first time. Her bedroom was comfortable and we snuggled until morning. The next day we ate breakfast at a beachside restaurant, followed by a long walk along the surf. She was from Myersville, Maryland, a country town noted for its elegant large farms, about an hour from Washington, DC. Her parents worked together: Chuck was a country doctor and Dottie was a nutritionist. Kristi had one sister, Karlynn, who was two years younger. All in all, her upbringing was a world apart from mine.

From the get-go, I had concerns about not only our ten-year age difference but how to reconcile my secret life with her. I could tell my feelings for her went much deeper than for any other woman I had dated, a phenomenon that was affirmed by how quickly things were advancing with us. I was torn between telling and showing her everything and keeping quiet. I had a huge fear bringing up my secret life and being rejected. I elected to open up to her only after moving into her place. One night while lounging around in the bedroom naked with the light on, I allowed her to finally see my tattoos that I had done such of a remarkable job of concealing up to this point. She was surprised and asked why I had done this to myself.

My explanation of the tattoos opened the way to share with her the saga of my closeted life. It wasn't a full recounting; I left some things out. But I did show her my suitcase and its contents of panties, skirts, dresses, and magazines so that she'd have a general idea of where I was coming from. But then I qualified everything by stating that all of this was behind me now. I stated that I was planning to jettison the suitcase and its contents, noting that this behavior was part and parcel of my past drug-addled world. It was a great speech, very convincing. I believed it myself because I had fallen so deeply in love and truly thought my secret life was now over for good, that from here on out I could live as just a normal guy. How much easier and saner my life would be! Still, a little voice urged caution. "Not so fast, think about the situation you're putting yourself, slow down, you're running away again." Did I listen? No. I couldn't listen. I *wouldn't* listen. Love is very powerful; it clouds judgment. I became lost in the sheer joy of loving Kristi.

That love soon made me leave San Diego and follow Kristi to Oregon. We moved in 1987 and got married there. The outdoors of the Northwest blew us away. We explored the amazing forests and scenic coast in addition to undertaking ambitious far-flung trips, like the three-week tour we did through Southeast Asia. These changes certainly improved my quality of life, but I was still drinking heavily and smoking pot to dull my true female self, which marriage and love had not diminished, as I hoped it would.

Being nature and travel lovers, in 1991 Kristi and I combined both passions and relocated to Costa Rica. We found a house in the hills outside the capital, San José, which afforded us open space and nature even as we commuted by bus into the city to work. Kristi taught English, and I got a job with a locally owned travel operator before I struck out on my own to launch Costa

Rica Incentives, a corporate tour company. It was an adventurous period, full of growth professionally. I brought sophisticated US travelers to a country that at the time had yet to draw many Americans. My chaperoning a group of wealthy cattlemen up a jungle river was a bit reminiscent of my fish camp guiding, only now I was the boss and much better paid. This demanding yet fulfilling business offset problems emerging in my marriage. Kristi and I rarely had sex anymore, and I worried about what would happen to us, even as I felt angry at and resentful toward Kristi for withholding affection. Our eventual return to Oregon happened in stages. First, while on a skiing trip that included a visit to Portland, I reconnected with the marketing director at the symphony. Fundraising was lagging, he said, before asking point-blank if I would like to be a consultant to help build up my old subscriber program. The compensation numbers he threw at me were double what I'd earned there previously. It was too irresistible, especially since I would still be able to travel back and forth to run Costa Rica Incentives.

Almost immediately upon my part-time return to Portland I began to slip with regard to my fidelity to Kristi. I didn't start using drugs but did resume phone sex and later began to seek out dominatrixes. There were times when I'd take an extended lunch hour to do these things or go after work. It was a form of cheating that I felt terrible about. It was one thing to indulge in these vices before I was married, but now the behaviors took on a new meaning. Several times I had to fight the urge to try and find crystal meth, compromising instead for an over-the-counter stimulant called ephedrine, also known as "poor man's speed." Though nowhere near as strong as meth, it got me high enough to do irrational things, and I was slowly overwhelmed by it. What saved me during this period was getting out of Portland often and returning to Costa Rica, where that stuff seemed a world away, because it was. After four years of living in Costa Rica, Kristi felt restless and increasingly dissatisfied with her teaching position. She pushed for us to return to Oregon for good, and I acquiesced. It was a bittersweet departure. I had become *tico*—native—and liked living there. I had grown accustomed to the lifestyle. I loved not having a car, riding the buses, my noon nap, the casualness and slower pace, the tropical weather, *tico* food, the outdoor market where we did our shopping, the gentleness of the Costa Rican people; all these things meant a lot and I became depressed over giving them up, these things we'd worked so hard for. We did bring back our German shepherd Tara, whom we had adopted from our neighbors. She was a great companion and no small consolation.

We were back in rural Oregon, in virtual forest, in fact. I loved it, and it wasn't long before all of our pets did too. They could now roam freely by day, though we kept Tara on a runner leash since she was inclined to chase our cats. I was so smitten by Tara. She was such a caring, loving, and loyal dog. I had no idea that the German shepherd breed had such wonderful attributes. She relished our daily walks in the forest. Once I took her on an especially long route where we came on an open, sunny meadow. She seemed so proud walking beside me, her chest out, ears pointed and alert, when she suddenly changed her gait into a regal trot. I was surprised by this, stopped, and lay down in the cool tall grass to let her explore this charming meadow. She was curious about everything but didn't go far and soon circled over and sat down by me. Good, loyal Tara, I thought. You are happier now than any other time in your life.

My own happiness faced a new threat: a mortgage. Under pressure from Kristi's parents, we bought our first house, an investment that didn't make sense to me but an argument I ultimately lost. We settled on a two-bedroom, one-bath place on an acre of land five miles outside the town of Vernonia, located forty-five miles northwest of Portland. My days now started before sunrise.

I left the house at 5 a.m. in order to stop in Saint Helens and swim laps at the municipal pool, in a building built during the Depression as part of the Works Project Administration, before driving on to the office. With my ninety-mile round trip commute, plus chores and everything else, it became routine for me to only get five to six hours of sleep a night. This schedule, coupled with my alcohol and pot habit and steadily increasing use of ephedrine, made me a wreck. I hid all this behavior from Kristi, which only increased my anxiety. On top of the house payment, we also had a new Toyota truck and a late model Subaru, both financed. Though Kristi found a really good job with the English Language Institute located on the campus of Pacific University in Forest Grove, I made all the payments each month, increasing the pressure on me to work more hours. My travel company, now named Costa Rica/Oregon Incentives, continued to attract groups, including VIP corporate types as well as nature buffs interested in exploring the tropical rainforest. To administer to the many operational details during the hours I was sharpest, I began doing this work while on the clock for the symphony. I felt bad about violating the trust I had with my supervisor. Yet he had no clue what was happening, and because I got away with it, I kept doing it.

One positive use of my energy, as well as Kristi's, was our joint involvement in the environmental movement. Our concern came about when we chanced to drive past a clear-cut on Mount Hood that looked so horrendous we felt enraged enough to take action. We joined not only the Portland Sierra Club but also the Cascadia Forest Alliance, which was more radical in scope and promoted direct actions such as sit-ins and tree sitting. Initially we focused on federal forests, but soon we got involved with state forests, specifically the Tillamook State Forest, which we lived on the edge of. Comprising 325,000 contiguous acres, it was the largest in the state. Logging companies had recently resumed clear-cutting here following terrible burns in the 1950s that were a result of unsafe logging practices. Now the mills were up and running again, and the logging interests wanted to decimate the restored grow-back. Kristi and I assumed the chair of the Tillamook State Forest Committee with the Sierra Club. Gradually, as our power grew and we recruited more members to the cause, more funding came our way. Our grand plan was to publish a book that would be called *50 Hikes in the Tillamook State Forest*. The hikes would range from easy strolls for families to difficult ascents for serious hikers. The idea behind the book was to show Portland residents what a gem of a forest lay at their back door, just twenty-five miles west of the city. We knew the undertaking could take several years to produce but committed ourselves to make it happen. We relied entirely on volunteers and although we obtained Sierra Club grants we also had to raise funds on our own. Our activism began to consume our free time to the point that I wondered why we were so obsessed with this project. At moments, Kristi sensed my misgivings, but I always acted like my dips in enthusiasm were no big deal. I didn't want to jeopardize this effort as it seemed to be keeping us together.

In addition to organizing fund-raisers, we formed the Tillamook Explorers. We undertook the grunt work of going deep into the forest to do GPS mapping of the trails and write narratives for each one. It was grueling work, and sometimes we had to go back repeatedly to get the mapping exactly right. Often it was just Kristi and me in our rain ponchos on muddy hillsides, since many of the initially gung-ho volunteers burned out as the project stretched on. We also cooperated with the Oregon Department of Forestry by helping the agency build new trails in the Tillamook. Though we saw them as the enemy, we wanted to foster better relations with them to demonstrate that the Sierra Club wasn't just a bunch of Portlanders who whined about logging but never ventured into the forest. I had no idea how hard it was to build a trail through a forest! On many occasions we argued with ODF employees about forest conservation even as we worked shoulder to shoulder, swinging our ax picks and hoes. With my knowledge of state forest issues and command of the proper terminology, I could stand my ground with the best of them. The ODF never really did like us, but they respected us. Our masterstroke in organizing was to form the Tillamook State Forest Coalition, an umbrella for other likeminded environmental organizations. This brought in new blood for our final push to finish the book. *50 Hikes in the Tillamook State Forest* became a reality—with an initial press run of ten thousand copies. There was a huge party at which Kristi was recognized for all the hard work she'd put into the effort. Without her, it never would have happened; she was the catalyst, the driver, the organizer, and motivator. I was extremely proud of and happy for her.

It was during one of these forest campaigns that I received a call from my mother, who had bad news. My father had suffered a massive heart attack and was in a coma. She asked that we come to Milwaukee straight away. I was shocked by this development, having had no idea his health was so poor, although there had been signs. Earlier in the year my dad told me on the phone that I had "turned out all right" and had done a good job with things. This very much surprised me; I thought I'd never hear such words from him. Then a $1,000 check arrived from him. I learned he'd mailed one out to each of us kids with a note telling us to enjoy— again, completely out of character. It seemed he was trying to make amends, albeit late, in his own awkward way. But he was barely seventy, so his dying never really entered my mind.

I broke the news to Kristi, whom I fully expected to come with me to Milwaukee. Incredibly, she refused, saying she had too much lesson planning, adding rather lamely that someone needed to stay in Oregon to take care of our pets. I saw these as weak excuses and was dumbfounded that she didn't want to travel with me, considering that this was it for my dad. I told her it would mean a lot to me if she were at my side, reminding her how hard it was for me to be with my family alone, having always struggled with them emotionally. But she was adamant about not going. She also mentioned the work with the state forest issue and the Sierra Club. Stunned, I left the living room and began packing my bag, wondering how a wife could be so cold as to refuse to be with her spouse during the death of a parent. I considered how she would react if the situation was reversed and it was one her parents who was dying. I almost made an issue of it but held back, not wanting to create conflict.

Less than twenty-four hours later, I stepped inside my old house in Greendale. Nothing had changed; my high school graduation picture still hung on the wall. My mother was sitting at the kitchen table as usual, with my brother, David, and my two sisters, Debbie and Karen. I was the last family member to arrive. There was a palpable awkwardness around the table, so I took the lead, saying that while we had all struggled to get along over the years, we should make an effort this one time to be nice to one another. "Dad is in a coma, dying," I said, "and we've come here to say goodbye to him." My mother started weeping, and we all seemed to be on the same page. I hoped it would hold throughout the ordeal that was coming, but of course it didn't.

The weather was blistering hot and humid for early June, so everyone wanted to be indoors with the central air conditioning running full blast. David and Karen were at each other's throats by the second day, to the point that I ended up finding myself a hotel nearby. There was no way I could stay in that house with them, plus the place brought back so many unpleasant memories that all I could think about was how to get away. Of course, once I was at the hotel I felt awful, like I was somehow abandoning the family. How I wished Kristi were with me! Enduring all the horrible childhood memories on my own was almost unbearable. At night I numbed myself with a twelve pack and plenty of pot, rounded out by unhealthy fast food.

Karen demanded a CAT scan be done before we disconnected the life support systems our father was hooked up to. This was carried out, and later that afternoon the doctor called to ask that we come to the hospital to review the results. Imagine my surprise when nobody wanted to go, not even Karen. I asked, "Why did we order this procedure if no one wants to hear the results?" My question was met with a collective stony silence. When I arrived alone at the hospital the doctor wanted to know where the rest of my family was. I had to tell her it was just me. She looked stunned, and then inquired about Karen, who had demanded the test. I simply said she didn't want to come. I was so infuriated with my family at this point.

The test results were all bad. The doctor showed me on the scans how my father's brain had swelled up against the skull, and she pointed out the dead brain tissue associated with his condition. There was no hope he'd come out of the coma; my father was effectively brain dead. The ICU medical staff believed it was time to stop treatment, and the doctor asked me when I wished to disconnect the life support system. Apparently it was up to me to make the decision, as I was the only one who showed up. However, I needed no clearer directive: it was time to say goodbye.

I went to my father's room and sat down and watched him breathe, made possible by a ventilator forcing air into his lungs. Through his thin hospital gown I could see his heart pumping, but again all due to a machine. His brain had nothing to do with anything keeping him alive. I observed him closely; it seemed like he was asleep, resting comfortably, and at peace. Getting up, I walked over to the window and gazed out, tears streaming down my face. I thought back through the years of all the good and bad things that happened between us: playing ball and going fishing, the physical abuse, those family vacations, the verbal abuse, kissing him goodnight, and the humiliations he put me through. Then it hit me that he'd never said "I love you" to me. I turned, alone in that room with him, stepped over to the bed and put my hands on his lower legs—I couldn't bring myself to hug him—and, sobbing, told him, "I love you, and I forgive you." Backing away, still crying, I wondered if there was any chance he could have heard me. Forgiving is the hardest thing to do as human beings and it was important to me that he understood what I'd done.

I returned to the house and shared the news with my family. My mother cried quietly as I helped her pick out his best suit for the burial. Next we went with my Uncle Harry to the funeral home to make the arrangements and select a coffin. It was decided he'd have a funeral mass at Saint Alphonsus, even though he'd stopped going to church decades ago. Of course, my old parish wanted a donation. I kept my mouth shut, despite my anger at the thought of being back inside that corrupt institution for my father's funeral. However, I didn't let go of the anger; I just redirected it at Kristi for deserting me when I needed her.

Though previously absent, the whole family gathered at the hospital early the next day and watched silently as the hospital staff prepared to switch off the life support unit. Then Steve, my brother-in-law, interrupted the process, announcing that he wanted to say something. Once the staff withdrew to give us privacy he pulled out a bottle of brandy and passed out shot glasses. After all were filled, we toasted my father. The brandy burned my throat, then my belly, but it sort of mellowed me. I proposed another toast, then a third. The room quickly smelled like a distillery.

What happened next shocked me. The staff turned off the heart machine and yet his heart kept beating. They turned off the lung machine and yet he kept breathing; then we were asked to leave so they could remove the feeding tube, a messy procedure, they said. The alcohol had taken hold of me and I protested. It seemed to me that our dad was trying to live without life support, and I wanted to be there with him. Telling me to let him go, my family gently led me away. Down the hall, however, I cried out, "No, this isn't right!" and raced back to my father. The feeding tube was already out and a nurse was injecting something into his IV. I asked what it was. Morphine, to help him relax, I was told. But I could tell that he was still breathing, although with labor, and I had this horrible thought that he wanted to live and not leave us. I glanced at the screen showing his vital signs and saw the needle gauges begin to drop rapidly as the massive dose of morphine hit him.

I was convinced that this was the routine method for the hospital, any hospital: get the loved ones out of the way if the patient doesn't die and use morphine to finish him off. My family returned to the room. Large tears welling up in my eyes dropped onto my father's chest. The needles dropped to zero. He was dead. The color in his face faded away and a peculiar odor came up, sort of like sweat mingled with a sickly sweetness. The whole event was so disturbing; I'd just witnessed the hospital take my father's life.

Later at the funeral home I met the director, the same man who had worked on my grandfather Jaja years earlier. After turning the suit over to him I had a strange compulsion come over me and blurted out, "May I see him?" Why did I say that? Did I want another private moment with him so I could truly cry? I felt like that was what I had wanted to do earlier but couldn't, so maybe now I'd be able to. The funeral director, who remembered me, explained it would be better to wait until he was ready for viewing. I let it go. But once back to my rental car, a child's mournful tears gushed out of me.

That evening I got extremely drunk at a bar. Not just any bar, but one that was owned by a cousin, and not just any cousin. She was the one who had run the ad in *Aggressive Women* almost thirty years ago. The bar was eponymously named Patty's Place. Seated at the counter I watched as Patty served the customers. She was friendly with everyone. "What'll you have?" she asked when she got to me. I ordered a boilermaker and tossed a $20 bill on the bar. When my drink came I said, "Thanks, cousin." The light dawned on her face and she slid the bill back, saying my money was no good here. She was true to her word; the next several hours I drank for free. Between customers we had chances to chat a bit, and I did my best to project plain old normal Dennis, just another guy at the bar. It was important to me, so soon after my father's death, that she didn't think of me as the same person who had responded to her dominatrix ad from years before, and after the booze loosened my tongue, I made an awkward but nonetheless convincing statement that the past does not reflect who we are today. She locked eyes with me and I stared back at her with a confident smile. I was such a good actor.

I stumbled out of there thinking how fake and phony I'd been, running away from my true self once again, pretending to be someone I wasn't.

The viewing time was limited to one hour prior to the mass, and when they closed the coffin, a curtain went up. I peeked around to observe the way they cranked the corpse down lower into the casket, so they could seal the lid. I watched my father slide from view, tears again in my eyes, and said goodbye to him in my own private way as he disappeared from my life forever.

A large crowd had turned out at Saint Alphonsus. This Catholic community I was born into obeyed the rote commands from the priest to stand, sit, kneel, read the Gospel, hear the Word, and be redeemed. When it came time for personal comments, my two nieces got up to read remembrances they'd written. The priest asked who else wished to speak. There was an awkward lull during which no one volunteered. The priest looked over at me desperately; as the oldest son it would've been appropriate for me to rise and say something—anything. But I couldn't do it. My feet were frozen and I couldn't move. So it was left to the priest. He spoke about my father's roses, which he had been very fond of growing, something I knew all too well, since it was me, the indentured servant, who had toiled for hours in the garden. I thought how sad it was that it had been left up to the priest to eulogize my father, and a wave of compassion for my father coursed through my body. I felt deeply sorry for him: he had been a very closed person and, I realized, a lonely person. I shut my eyes and prayed to the universe not to let me die a lonely person. The need to avoid such a fate was the lesson I took away that day.

I was one of the pallbearers who hoisted and walked the casket to the waiting hearse. Since my parents' house was on the way to the cemetery, I asked the funeral director if we could drive past it, and he readily agreed. I wanted my dad to see his house one more time. He had put years of hard work into it, so one last hurrah seemed fitting. At the cemetery we gathered around the coffin as it was set down next to his final resting spot and said our farewells. My mother's grave was already purchased and right beside his for when her time came. It all seemed so surreal to me.

There was a traditional Polish wake at a nearby restaurant with an open bar, homemade sausage, cooked ham, Polish salads, hard rolls, borsch, all of which elicited a flood of memories. I saw relatives I hadn't seen in decades, each one looking much older and all, I noticed, still hard-core drinkers. Uncle Teddy, who was eleven years older than my dad, showed up in a wheelchair. He'd lost both of his legs to diabetes. I helped wheel him up to the bar when he needed another brandy. My Uncle Ervin, a notorious boozer, commented how he wished that he could fill up his walking cane with brandy. I sat with Uncle Frank and Aunt Dorothy, the pair I had lived with when I first moved to Southern California. During our amiable chat my mind flashed back to that suitcase full of my girl clothes and my certainty that my aunt had opened it and discovered my secret. How much longer would my secret life remain just that, I wondered. Was it worth it to remain in the closet for the rest of my life, or would I eventually find my way to the brightness of the day?

$\mathcal{A}$ horrible thing happened on my return home to Oregon. Right when I needed unconditional support following the stress of my father's passing, Kristi announced that because she had four days off from work, she wanted to go camping. I didn't have any time off and couldn't go, so instead of postponing the trip she went for a jaunt in the Cascades with her sister. Unbeknownst to her, I was intensely craving crystal meth, and her departure left me in a very vulnerable situation. She was gone barely a few hours when I hopped into my truck and headed into Portland, where I knew someone who would likely have what I wanted. I was right. After making my purchase I rushed back to my truck, poured a generous amount of the drug into a bottle of water, and lustfully watched it slowly twist down, dissolving and leaving a meth trail.

Before chugging down the mixture, I paused. There was still time to not do this, I told myself. After all, it's been more than fourteen years since you've done crystal meth, it's highly addictive, and it could ruin your marriage, your health; a lot of things could go very wrong. But then I thought of the sexual activity that was so much a part of the drug experience for me. I hadn't had sex in forever, it seemed, and this stuff would get me going. I envisioned shopping for panties, dress shopping, making a fool of myself in front of salesgirls, getting my hair done sissy-like, maybe even having my eyebrows waxed and arched. I imagined storming into adult bookstores and loading up on fem-dom porn—which would be so exciting after the many years of depriving myself. All my past desires came thundering back and I shut my eyes and drank the concoction. There was so much crystal in the water that it numbed my throat, and the bitter taste was hard to keep down.

I drove around waiting for the effects to kick in; it didn't take long. The drug hit me like a ton of bricks, and, not having been this high for so long, it was pure ecstasy. My God, it was 1983 again! All I could think about was engaging my sexual feelings. I pulled into the parking lot of an adult bookstore that advertised live shows. I walked through the door and saw a woman dressed in very sexy lingerie seated by a small stage that had a privacy curtain. She kind of laughed at me, which made me feel submissive. "You're tweaking," she said. With eyes cast down, I replied, "What does that mean, mistress?" Now she really laughed, telling me I was naughty being so high on meth. With the definition of *tweaking* clear, I wandered over to the magazine area, quickly zeroing in on any issues that catered to my fetish.

I was so high I never made it back to Vernonia that night. Instead, I drove around until dawn, going to adult bookstores and even drugstores to browse women's fashion magazines. A nagging voice tried warning me that I was out of control: "Just go home now. You have plenty of porn; enjoy yourself all you want with what you already have." But I couldn't stop myself. Time became completely irrelevant and after taking more meth and smoking some weed, I went shopping as soon as the malls opened. I must have looked like a wreck, having been up all night, and I did my best to make sure the sales girls knew the panties, dresses, garters, and stockings were for me. I wanted them to laugh at me, which they did. I spent a huge amount of money and didn't care. One stop was at a beauty salon. I intended to really feminize myself: a body wax, brows made pencil thin, a humiliating girly perm, maybe even permanent tattoo eyeliner, something I'd heard was the latest rage.

But the deep appeal of this fantasy was challenged by an intense urge to masturbate. I made the choice to return home, telling myself it would be only for a little while before I headed out to a salon. This decision saved me because I never, in the next day and half, left the house. I simply could not stop taking more meth—until it was all gone—smoking a ton of weed, and masturbating as I paged through my new porn, all while dressed up and wearing sloppily applied makeup. Like so many years before, I looked like a fright: dripping in sweat, no sleep, no food, and very little water. The pets stayed clear of me; they could sense I was out of control. Day turned to night, and then again. I finally dozed off but woke a few hours later, ready to do more drugs and pore over more still-unopened magazines.

A mammoth orgasm brought me back to quasi-reality. I was now out of meth. I was only forty-five miles from Portland, where there was more, but my four days were up; Kristi would be home soon. I lay there panting and sweating, needing water, food, and rest. No time for any of that—I had to clean up, hide things, be ready to lie about what I did while she was away, and act like everything was normal. The bedroom was a disaster zone, reeking of pot, excessive body odor, and, worse, the unmistakable odor of inhalants. The sheets and pillowcases were damp with my sweat, and when I looked at myself in the mirror, I beheld a corpse from hell. How could I have let things get so out of control?

Guilt came home to roost hard. But then I had a delirious thought: why not come clean about the whole episode? Why not leave everything out and let Kristi see what had happened? I was backsliding into who I was before I was married; it was a horrible setback. Yet even as I recognized this truth, in the back of mind there was my addiction reasserting itself, a voice urging me to clean up, repack the truck, drive to Portland, get more meth, and forget about Kristi. You can be high, tweak more, get a hotel room, and finish the job by going to a beauty salon. Your guilt trip will go away! "Do it," the voice told me. "Do it *now!*"

I began to tidy up with that very plan of action in mind. I would run out on Kristi . . . and maybe never come back. I had plenty of credit cards and would be able to stay high quite a long time, tweaking my brains out. I changed the sheets, fed the pets, and stepped into the shower. As the water cleaned away days' worth of perspiration and smeared makeup, I thought of Kristi, our pets, our home, our life together all of these years: our first meeting in San Diego, the move to Oregon, our wedding and backpacking honeymoon, our big trip to Southeast Asia, the many adventures we had living in Costa Rica. . . . Shortly I found myself sobbing, overcome by tremendous sadness. I still loved Kristi over everything; I couldn't leave her like this.

The pull of meth addiction is so strong that in the very next minute I was once again scheming. I wanted so badly not to purge my new clothing and magazines. Still under the influence, I resolved to rent a storage shed where I could put everything, one large enough to fit a dresser, with a mirror and chair, that I could set up just right. I could visit the storage unit, do meth in there, and play with my things—Kristi would never be the wiser. I decided I'd make this happen the following day. This new fantasy made me want more meth immediately. I paced anxiously, very tempted to leave that minute for more drugs. I understand better now why I so wanted the meth (aside from the fact that the pull of my addiction was so overpowering): being high let me feel sexual without the guilt.

In the end I didn't resupply. When Kristi arrived early that evening excited to tell me all about her trip I struggled to appear interested. I was physically and emotionally drained, crashing hard as the last of the meth left my body. Feigning illness in order to be alone, I crept off to bed and pretended to sleep. She must've sensed something was off, for when she came to bed she asked if I was awake. I jumped to conclusions: oh, my god, she wants to have sex! Now, after not wanting it for so long! Only it was impossible now; I was a wasted tweaker only able to imagine the kind of sex that was packed away out in the wood shed. I rolled away from her and tried to fall sleep. It was cruel and selfish of me. I wanted to tell her what had happened these last four days but lacked the courage to speak honestly with my wife, who was still my best friend. Her last comment was about the strange odor; she could smell the inhalant. I lied, saying the cats had sprayed in the room so I used some deodorizer.

The next morning, a Saturday, I was somewhat revived and back to craving meth. I devised a plan that would allow me to get high for the whole weekend, without Kristi's knowledge. If I called ahead for the meth, the trip into Portland would be more productive, time-wise. And I could easily tell Kristi I had to go into the symphony office. Taking this first step, I waited until I thought she was out in the garden and made the call. Unknown to me, she'd come back inside as I was talking. She overheard "meth" and I don't know what else. Enough, it turned out, that after I hung up, I found her crying at the kitchen table. She looked at me imploringly, desperately, saying only, "I don't know who you are." Her tears tore at the very foundation of my being but instead of coming clean, I said, "I don't know what you mean. I was only joking around on the phone with my printer in the symphony office, that's all it was."

She wanted to believe me so much that she did. Once I thought I'd calmed her down, she asked if I'd been cheating on her. This I could honestly deny, except that my actions during the past four days were akin to cheating, just not in any way she could've imagined. Regardless, seeing her cry and looking so down and defeated broke my heart. I didn't go into Portland that day, never got the storage unit, and I swore off meth. The addiction was broken, I thought. Still, I hadn't done anything to resolve the growing rift in our marriage. Several days later I threw everything I'd bought during my tweaking binge into a dumpster, like I'd done so many other times in my life. I felt foreboding afterward. That little voice deep down inside kept repeating, "Do it again, do it now, do it again, do it now!"

Kauai and Tribeca, 2008, and Oregon, 2002

James Westby called and delivered the good news while I was in Hawaii, but I didn't grasp its significance right away. After hanging up the phone I went right back to enjoying my two-month stay at the Mermaid House, a historic home located on the north shore of Kauai. I resumed my life of running, swimming, snorkeling, boogie boarding, sun bathing, stargazing on the beach, and firing up the barbecue each night to grill fresh-caught fish. I was three years removed from my sex reassignment surgery in Bangkok and had blossomed into the beautiful, confident woman I always knew I could be. My self-esteem had shot up. I loved who I was, feeling secure and safe in my own person for the first time in my life.

This high-on-life attitude was such a contrast to my outlook a few years earlier. I had been so broke that I was sleeping in an unheated garage. That was in Portland, where I returned to live soon after arriving back in New York following my surgery. So much had changed since those hand-to-mouth days. Now I rented a beautiful condo in the heart of Portland's revitalized downtown. The floor-to-ceiling windows in my spacious tenth-floor unit in a gorgeous new building gave a commanding view of the city and stunning vistas of glacier-covered Mount Saint Helens, Mount Rainier, and Mount Adams. These peaks were more than a mere pretty backdrop. I had hiked on their slopes and their beauty had inspired me personally, at times encouraging me to be environmentally active and at others simply to keep on living through rough times. After getting back on my feet and settling old debts, I'd bought new furniture, financed a newer-model car, and bought a new wardrobe that I painstakingly put together. But best of all, I was living my life free of any alcohol or hard drugs. No more speed, hidden suitcases, or insecurity about who I was. I had arrived and didn't think things could get much better.

James Westby was the director of an indie film, *The Auteur*, in which I had played a minor role. I originally met him and the producer, Byrd McDonald, at a party a year prior; I was in their work studio when they asked me if I would be interested in being cast in their project. I was speechless for a moment and had to calm myself down before saying yes. The writer, it turned out, was creating a character for me specifically. I couldn't believe what I was hearing. When told I would still have to go through the audition process, I of course said that would be fine. For the next couple of weeks I got up for my early morning run and swim not knowing how I was doing it. I had a smile plastered on my face as I daydreamed my way through my five-kilometer jog on the track and my one-mile swim at the health club. The rest of the day I remained buoyed by this same great feeling. My karma was such that my entire life now seemed to have limitless possibilities. It wasn't just the offer of the movie role. Everything I touched turned to gold. I routinely got compliments on my appearance, and many new acquaintances wanted to get together and hang out. Why? Because I was finally living an authentic life and it showed.

Six years back everything had begun to seriously change. Kristi had moved to New Zealand to accept a teaching position at the

University of Canterbury in Christchurch, the plan being for me to stay behind and sell the house before joining her for our next overseas live-work adventure. But instead, I seized on her absence to begin to transition. After decades of hiding who I really was, I finally took the first therapeutic step: what's called real-life experience, or RLE. I wanted to do this right, to make certain that becoming a woman would work for me. RLE demands that you live for at least one year, full-time, as a member of your new chosen gender. Part of me, actually most of me, thought this would be a breeze. After all, I had a lifetime of experience in dressing, doing makeup, painting nails, wearing wigs, shopping, and following fashion styles. I felt sure I would skate right through this trial period of living my new life. I was never so wrong. There's a huge difference between hiding out in a hotel room pretending to be a woman and trying to fit in as one out in society. I was shocked to discover how difficult this was. To start with, there was the simple fact that I was out in public, dressed, and actually caring what others thought of me. No longer was my aim to get off on people laughing at me— the old humiliation turn-on routine. Now I desperately wanted to "pass." Everything about myself made me self-conscious: my height, weight, posture, male voice, facial hair, body hair, upper shoulders, thicker arms, my walk, gait, hips, my makeup, clothes, accessories, my eye contact with others, and most important, how I felt projecting overall as female.

It was sensory overload of the highest order, and it became the greatest challenge of my life.

Thinking I'd seen it all and overcome so much—having reached this crossroads without ending up dead in the street from a gunshot wound that evening in Point Loma or of an overdose in some seedy motel room surrounded by fetish magazines—what could possibly be left to stop me now from fully transitioning? Nothing, I thought, until RLE came along. For the first time in my years of wanting to be a woman, there was a doubt in my mind that I did not want it bad enough.

"Can I actually do this?" I kept asking myself.

The answer was: I had to. I had to find a way. So the actor in me focused; this would be my most important role. A real-life part, not an onstage character, not a fantasy in my head. *Real.* I was going to have to work each and every day at passing as a woman, concentrate on my self-confidence and self-esteem, all to convince the public to believe in me so that I could believe in myself. RLE, I already knew, defeats many who think they want to transition. The experience changes their minds because they realize they lack the willingness to put the required work into it. I wanted sex reassignment surgery at all costs; it was a goal I was willing to knock myself out for. Which I did. But it was a tough year made even tougher by the fact that for the first half of it I fully relapsed into crystal meth addiction. That tweaker side of me who had reemerged during the four-day binge after my father's funeral returned the very same day Kristi left for New Zealand.

The day arrived for my movie audition. I only became nervous when I showed up to the studio and saw the camera set up to videotape me onstage. There were a half-dozen unfamiliar people present; I knew just the director. Still, I summoned my acting experience from my days in San Diego and began reading the lines from the script. My theater work came flooding back, and I handled the basic stage movements flawlessly. Moreover, I had a platform of confidence in the knowledge that both the director and producer had pretty much indicated that the audition was a formality, since the part had been written with me in mind. Still, as I left the stage, I had misgivings. Chiefly, the body language of the casting director gave me the uneasy feeling she didn't care much for my performance. I put the concern out of my head, pumped up again over this exciting opportunity. A week passed without any word from anyone connected to the project. Had they forgotten about me? When I reached out to the director, I discovered the casting director had chosen someone else for my role. I was shocked—and crushed—but, luckily, the disappointment was only temporarily. I had come too far in my "new life," as I had started calling it, to let a little rejection for a movie pull me down. Still, I wrote a passionate email to the producer to let him know how sorry I was not to be cast. My forthright note saved the day. The producer, touched by my words, replied, stating that I was back in the film. The turnabout was all thanks to the director, who had the right to cast one person independently of the casting company. I was given a part that an actor from California had declined to take.

The first time I met my RLE transition coach in Portland I thought it was a total waste of time. I sat opposite a diminutive, frail-looking old woman. I was supposed to pay $75 an hour to have her tell me how to live as a woman? Actually, she wasn't going to tell me anything, she promptly explained. It was up to me to find things out and to ask her questions. She neither wished to dissuade me nor convince me of anything. "If this is what you want," she said, "it's yours to take. I'm only here to show you the road." She smiled. "You have to do the walking, not me." I left her office, where I had at least felt safe, back out to the street, where I sure as hell didn't. I walked briskly and uneasily toward my car, thinking everyone saw only a man walking in a dress, wearing a wig, in bad makeup, hunched over and unable to look anyone in the eye.

I drove back out to my country home and cried. I lived in an area that was backward, not free thinking or accepting of anything different. I lacked the courage to go into Vernonia and shop at the local grocery store because everyone there knew me, and I couldn't bear the thought of what they'd think seeing me in my new life as Denise. I started avoiding the few neighbors I had and kept to myself. It became evident that living out there was not healthy for me any longer and I knew moving into the city was a foregone conclusion. The sad part was that I truly liked the country and loved the freedom to roam it gave my pets. I wanted even more to preserve this for them without Kristi around, for I relied entirely on them for unconditional love. Humans have the same capacity for love but we drive it out of ourselves as if it were a toxic substance, rejecting who we are, what we were meant to be: caring, positive beings, offering total love to each other. My pets reminded me of this every day, and one of the most difficult experiences of these months was my painful parting with Spunky, a black lab I brought home one day to fill the void after our German shepherd, Tara, died. Spunky was to travel to New Zealand to be reunited with Kristi.

The shooting of my scenes took place during one long evening inside my condo with the city lights of Portland as a backdrop. It took about five hours, and with the hot lights I was drenched in sweat by the end. In fact, the makeup artist had to constantly refresh my face as my mascara dripped. My character was Margaret Le Plage, who was the president of the Arturo Domingo Fan Club, Arturo being the main character in the comedic film. My role was small but I did have the opening line, which thrilled me. For a while afterward I heard nothing. It seemed the editing was taking forever. And though I was in touch with both the director and producer during the next year because we were friends, I didn't ask too often about the movie. I knew they were busy working on it.

Then in January 2008, I took off to Hawaii for a two-month stay to escape the damp, gray Portland winter. *The Auteur* was in a far recess of my mind until that phone call from the director. He sounded excited and unusually verbal. "Denise," he said breathlessly, "the film was selected to appear at the Tribeca Film Festival." It was? I had never heard of the event and had no clue of its prestige. Upon returning to Portland I got the chance to look it up. The first image that popped up on the festival's website was a picture of Robert De Niro, the event's founder. That cinched it—I was headed to New York.

Eager to immerse myself, I purchased a platinum pass so I'd be able to attend all the VIP events and parties. I wanted to return to New York in style. I had lived there for the months right before and right after my surgery in Bangkok. Those were trying times. Frankly, New York had kicked my rear end. I held no grudge; it was just how the city can be for any newcomer. And now I was ready for a victory lap. I wanted to show the city what a strong and confident person I'd become. Maybe I didn't "make it" there, as the song goes, but I had made it on my terms, and here I was an actress in a film participating in one of its most prestigious cultural events to boot. I couldn't wait to light up the festival and city. It was the old story of a girl with dreams of making a splash, only it had taken me just a little longer.

A few months into RLE, my therapist asked me out of the blue if I felt ready to start hormone replacement therapy, or HRT. I knew about HRT. I had voraciously read everything about how it worked, what it did, the expectations, side effects, and dangers. I was more than book smart on the topic. I had actually already gone online and preordered enough estrogen to change the sex of an elephant and was just waiting for her to suggest this next step. HRT is a big deal, a major milestone in the transition process. Expectations are high. Some think it's a wonder drug. But merely taking estrogen (in tandem with an antiandrogen drug to curtail and repress testosterone production in the testicles) does not make you a woman.

I opted for estrogen patches and the antiandrogen pill Androcur. It took a few weeks to observe noticeable changes, many of them negative. My libido nose-dived, I had trouble sleeping, I was moody and at times even depressed. The estrogen patches weren't easy to work with, but I was stuck with them since I had purchased such a huge supply and didn't have the cash to switch to injections.

My decreased libido was a problem. I desperately wanted to keep masturbating but could no longer get release. Even going at it for hours with all the usual props—fem-dom magazines, inhalants, clothes, phone sex—produced nothing.

I couldn't solely blame the estrogen. Neither my RLE counselor nor anybody else knew that I had relapsed. After leaving Kristi at the airport for the first leg of her flight to Christchurch, I immediately scored some crystal meth. Perhaps it was inevitable. With my wife out of the picture I was free to act out, to pick up where I had left off during my binge five years earlier. Rushing home, I diluted the powder in water, drank it down, and without wasting any time hopped back in my truck and drove to Portland armed with my credit cards. Halfway to town the crystal hit me, and the floodgates opened. I went straight to a mall and began buying intimate apparel, mountains of it, strolling up to the cash register and getting off on the strange stares and smiles the sales girls lavished on me. Next I visited a couple of porn shops, buying boxes full of magazines and bottles of inhalants. Then it was off to a supermarket to pick up the latest women's magazines for tips on fashion and beauty. I arrived home to Vernonia after midnight, whereupon I changed into my new clothes, smoked pot, began browsing my magazines and masturbating as I sniffed inhalants. Around dawn I showered, took more crystal—mixed into coffee this time—and drove back to Portland to a women-owned tattoo shop. This was going to be major. I had one large tattoo inked on my left upper leg that said PANTY TRAINED SUBMISSIVE MISS, with the female symbol in the center, and on my right upper leg one that said I LIKE TO WEAR PANTIES AND DRESSES AND BE A WANKING FOOL FOR FEM DOMS. The session lasted hours yet I was so high I didn't feel a thing. When the tattoos were complete the artist surveyed her work and laughed, saying, "Now you are marked again."

My new tattoos were humiliating, to be sure, but no one could see them. I needed to alter my appearance in a more dramatic way, I thought, and briefly toyed with the idea of having my head shaved and the word *Fool* tattooed across my forehead in bold capital letters. How shocking that would be! Everyone would know who I really was. But a saner voice, belonging to Denise, talked me into getting permanent makeup instead, for the day when I quit meth. The results would make going back into the closet very hard. I followed through on this, using credit cards to pay to have my eyes done with liner and shadow, my lips with liner and a filler, and my cheeks with rouge. It was an involved and painful process, requiring three different tattoo makeup specialists. In the end, however, my makeup looked beautiful. I also got laser treatment for my beard, which was also quite costly. Several months into RLE, I drove to the Goodwill and gave away the rest of my male clothes. How ironic. After all these years, it was finally the male clothes that were getting purged.

Sexually, I kept raising the bar. Soon my regular visits to the private adult "jack shacks" where I played being the submissive in domination sessions weren't enough. I searched the Internet for bigger dungeons, more professional dominatrixes, and began flying to places like New York and Los Angeles to seek out the "fem-dom lifestyle." This had become possible because of major changes at my employer, the symphony. Just prior to my drug relapse, new upper management came onboard. A complete restructuring occurred, and for the first time in my many years there I became unhappy. Though I survived a personnel shakeup, I declined the new position offered to me and accepted a severance package that included unemployment benefits. This payout, along with the abuse of my credit cards, allowed me to pursue my dream of becoming a full-time slave as well as to spend freely on the other habits I had developed.

It got very extreme. I became obsessed with an organization in the Czech Republic called the Other World Kingdom, or OWK for short. It was advertised as "the Private State of Supreme Women." This all-female dominatrix society accepted full-time male slaves for a price, and I was in contact with them about becoming one for an entire year. It worked like this: upon arrival to the kingdom, a new recruit had to turn over his passport and money and will himself to them as their complete slave. I agonized over this tantalizing opportunity for weeks. So much of me wanted to pursue being a full-time slave but doing so would mean being left with no money for my transition. In the end I chose to save the money for my sex reassignment surgery. Surgery remained the ultimate goal of my life; nothing had changed from that day long ago on the dock at my grandparents' cottage. This was the only rational decision I made during my relapse period.

The brand-new Greenwich Hotel, owned by Robert De Niro himself, in the heart of Tribeca, became my home for eleven days in February 2008. One evening, the front desk called and invited me down to a cocktail reception hosted by the Chanel Fragrance brand. I threw on a cute black dress and appeared there in five minutes. My hair and makeup were perfect because every day at 2 p.m. I went to Blow, a salon not far from my hotel. The stylists there were fantastic. Each day during the festival I got an updo and a makeover. I would leave the salon around four, ready for anything the Tribeca Film Festival could throw at me. I looked stunning and was so thrilled to finally have arrived as Denise in such a wonderful way and in one of the most spectacular cities in the world.

At the opening night bash I did my best to be noticed, making my way around the room with a club soda in hand, shoulders thrown back, walking tall, as I caught people's eyes and struck up casual conversations. It was an effort working that ballroom floor, but I looked glamorous in my dress, heels, jewelry, and salon-perfect makeup and hair. Not using alcohol to socialize was still a new experience; I was accustomed to getting loaded on booze, pot, and oftentimes whatever drug du jour happened to be around. Tribeca was a test. Like, for example, when I noticed the bartender put gin in my club soda by mistake and for a moment was tempted to take it. But I held firm and politely asked him to redo my drink. Right as I walked away I got a glimpse of Tina Fey. I almost approached her to give her one of the cards I had had specially made for the festival bearing my name, the film's title, and my contact information. She was very engaged with people she obviously knew, though, and it didn't seem appropriate.

Still, I wasn't lacking in nerve. I handed out eight cards that evening to strangers I chatted with, figuring, in this business you never know who might help you. "Yes, I'm here for Tribeca, and I'm an actress in *The Auteur*, which made the festival," I proudly declared. A couple of hours later, as I was helping myself at the coffee and chocolate island, a very nice man struck up a conversation with me. He seemed interested in the movie, and we talked about the festival. One of his close friends, he revealed, was the president of MGM. His partner then joined us and after talking some more I decided to out myself. They were shocked, saying they had no idea. "We noticed you several times," they said. "We thought you looked like Russian royalty, a baroness." They told me I looked absolutely beautiful and was the center of attention wherever I walked. In the cab on the way back to the hotel I had the biggest smile on my face. I had completed my victory lap, and the festival had only just begun.

The première of *The Auteur* was at hand. I knew from other screenings that week to expect a media reception. When I arrived at the theater in the East Village, the entire cast was there, but I became shy because I wasn't the star and was not sure if I belonged on the red carpet. The producer pulled me by the arm. "Come join us," he insisted. The cameras began flashing. It was an onslaught but I was ready, flashing my smile that showed off perfect white teeth, a far cry from their unsightly decayed condition a few years back, after meth had destroyed them. Further down the red carpet, I suddenly faced a television camera. A reporter started asking me questions about the movie and my part in it. I never missed a beat, saying that *The Auteur* had all the winning ingredients for a successful run: a great story, lots of humor, brilliant acting, and great music. I named my character, Margaret LaPlage, the president of Arturo Domingo's fan club. Moments later, I caught my breath, thinking, "Look at you, Denise! Look how far you've come these past four years."

The theater was packed, and when my opening line happened, many cast mates and friends in attendance whooped and cheered. I flushed and did so again after my name came onscreen during the opening credits. I had never felt more proud of myself. After all the struggles beginning so long ago, my life had opened up, exceeding my expectations and dreams. This glamorous event was such a contrast to my last time in New York. That had been a bittersweet period. I was broke after having spent every cent I had on my sex reassignment surgery. Yet I was still so happy. If I woke up fretting about money, all I had to do was put my hand down on my new made in Thailand vagina and a wide smile would spread across my face and my worries would wash away. One evening during the festival I slipped on some ice and went down hard, spilling the contents of my purse. The fall triggered a memory of a horribly cold night in the East Village when I was alone with just my Metro card and twenty-three cents—not even enough to make a phone call. So much had changed. I was Denise now. I was alcohol and drug free. I had become so strong and sure of myself, and I was certain that nothing could shake me. I laughed as I lay splayed out on that icy sidewalk.

Kristi called frequently from New Zealand and was beginning to suspect that something wasn't right. I had been left in charge of trying to sell our house, a chore that brought problems I could only barely handle in my condition. Far worse was the job of getting our dog Spunky ready for the long trip to New Zealand. What made it so difficult was knowing I would never be joining Kristi or Spunky there. Meth addiction had so completely changed me that I was fully ready to give up Kristi, our life together, and the opportunity of a lifetime to live in beautiful, prosperous New Zealand. I had traded all of this on the single hope of becoming Denise.

My last weeks with Spunky were doubly heartbreaking, as he was the only being left who loved me unconditionally. I might be passed out for a few hours from a drug-induced haze, but he would lie next to me and lick my face. At such low points, he became everything to me: my last connection to humanity. I also had to contend with our two remaining cats, Mira and Airport. Kristi and I had decided that it was too expensive to fly them to New Zealand, so it fell on me to do the dirty work of finding them a new home. I felt like I was betraying them; they trusted me so much. Fortunately, I found a woman willing to take both. Even so, the ride into Portland with them in their carriers was an ordeal. I cried all the way and sat parked outside their new home and cried some more. The only way I could cope with the experience was to race home and get high. Meth robs you of all goodness; it turns you into a self-centered, glutinous robot, void of any feeling, any caring, any hope.

Given my deteriorated physical state, it was difficult to walk Spunky; his imminent departure, however, kept me from slacking off. I took him on the Vernonia Linear Trail and let him loose. He would quickly disappear, tearing into the forest. Eventually he'd come running back, tongue hanging out, tail wagging, looking up at me with his doggy smile, ready to resume our walk while remaining alert to any new scent or interesting thing to explore. Back at the house I'd watch as he lapped up water from his bowl, drooling everywhere. I would lie down on the floor and cover my face so he couldn't scratch me as he burrowed in to lick me, a routine we had that made me laugh nonstop. These moments were the only times in my drug-addled state when I ever felt any joy.

Getting him travel-ready was very costly, and I was required to accompany him to LA for his connecting flight to Christchurch. I worked with a local veterinarian who ran tests and got him the inoculations he needed. This vet and his staff had known Kristi and me for many years. I was sure they noticed my physical changes and were wondering how much Kristi knew. I was grateful they had only our local phone number and no way to contact her. As Spunky's departure date neared, I became so distraught I seriously considered abandoning the house and keeping him. We could drive off in my truck and disappear, start a new life where no one could find us. But I knew I couldn't carry through on such a plan; Spunky deserved a full, active life with someone who would love him day in and day out. My addiction meant I could not deliver on that. During our last night together he slept with me in our hotel room in Los Angeles. Early the next morning I took him into the transfer area at the airport. We had an extra thirty minutes, so I took him for a walk, his last in the United States. Once he reached Christchurch, there would be a thirty-day quarantine, but Kristi would be able to visit him daily. The final minutes of our walk together were terrible. I was bawling and Spunky kept looking up at me forlornly, which made me cry harder. Again I was seized by the idea of calling the whole thing off and running away with Spunky to start a new life someplace. It took everything I had left in me to get him on that flight to New Zealand.

Back in Vernonia, the house seemed eerily empty. Kristi was still clueless about what was really going on. Whenever she called, I managed to act like all was well; I listened patiently to news about her good life in her new far-off place. Soon, Spunky was out of quarantine and Kristi told me how quickly he was adjusting to living at the beach. Instead of forests, he was now darting off into the sand dunes of the South Pacific. Each time I hung up the phone I cried with a mix of sadness at the thought of never seeing either of them again and gladness that at least they were together. Meanwhile, I lowered the price on the house. A new real estate agent was determined to sell the place and ignored the way I looked and acted. I was a freakish mess, looking the worse for wear from spending the bulk of my days and nights with some newfound tweaker buddies. They were totally untrustworthy but company nonetheless.

I cleared out the house, giving away what I could and trashing the rest. There was so much we'd accumulated over the years that the job felt overwhelming. I managed to ship ten boxes of personal stuff that I knew Kristi would want to her parents in Maryland and then brought in a dumpster for what was left. After five days it was full to the brim. All that remained was the futon, a pillow, and blankets. The futon was like me: dirty, stained, depressed in the middle, and caked with dried semen and salty dried sweat. My meth nightmare seemed to have no end—or only one possible ending: death. I could feel death getting closer. It seemed to me that I was powerless against it, and I began to think maybe this was the best way for me. I was losing everything, and soon there would be nothing.

Meth had undone me totally, yet as I would discover, this undoing was what gave me the courage to not just survive but to overcome and thrive. Something changed. Out of the black nothingness, I rallied. Where that strength came from I'll never know.

The first thing I did was try to use less meth each day, despite frequent setbacks. Gradually things improved. My mind cleared enough that I found the motivation to look for a place to live in Portland. I was very afraid I would not be able to accomplish this, since it had been years since I had lived with roommates and I wondered how I could possibly fit in anyplace. I was forty-eight, well above the average age of people sharing a house. I decided to restrict myself to listings advertising for a lesbian roommate. I figured that's what I was now, a lesbian, for I continued to like women. I was queer but not queer. Whatever I was, I felt like I belonged in an all-women household.

Erin and Joyce lived in a huge old house in northeast Portland: three bedrooms, one bath, a big front porch, a nice lesbian kitchen well stocked with dishware and organic food. Both women were in their early twenties—and hot. My exposure to the queer world was limited, and so I had no idea lesbians could be so sexy. All I was thinking during my interview with them was if this is lesbianism, then give me more of it! I was totally open with them about my ongoing RLE and my future SRS. As for being a crystal meth addict, I didn't mention anything about that. Oh, just a minor detail, I convinced myself. Indeed, the possibility of once and for all living as a woman was so empowering that I returned that night to Vernonia and flushed my considerable supply of crystal meth down the toilet. In one flush I'd done the unthinkable, separating myself from my addiction. Seconds later, regret seized hold of me. "How could you possibly be so stupid?" the meth-addict side of me said. "Erin and Joyce are interviewing at least five other candidates. You're not going to get that place. You're too old, you can't relate to them; you're a loser and an addict." But then the clean side of me said, "Now you have everything; you've taken the first step to quitting. Believe in yourself, stay true to who you really are, and the goodness that is within you shall prevail." I smiled as I gazed in the mirror, taking in my drawn, wrinkled, faded face. I smiled again and saw my worn-down teeth and sore gums. After another smile of acceptance I stepped into the bedroom, collapsed on my filthy futon and fell into a deep, dreamless sleep, not waking for two days.

$\mathcal{A}$t the closing night party for the film festival I was hoping for a good night working the crowd and handing out my card. I saw more familiar faces and was happy the festival was at an end. I was getting tired of being out all night, every night. I was also relieved to be done dropping money at Blow Salon and glad to be checking out of the expensive Greenwich Hotel the next morning. Having money in New York was a new experience. What I learned was, everything in New York is expensive when you have money because when you have it you just spend it. I noticed celebrities in the crowd, including De Niro himself. With his bodyguards close by, he was unapproachable. I was staring over toward him when suddenly there was a tap on my shoulder and I turned around to see a photographer standing with an assistant. "Excuse me," he said, "but you're in *The Auteur*, aren't you?" I smiled and said yes, and he asked for permission to take my photo. I noticed the camera was rather large but didn't think much of it and gave his assistant the spelling of my name. The following morning as I was preparing to check out of my hotel, a fellow cast member called to tell me my photograph had appeared in *USA Today*. I was so delighted that I interrupted my packing to go online to see for myself. There I was in all my glory at the wrap party of the Tribeca Film Festival. A caption correctly identified me: Denise Chanterelle DuBois. "Yes," I said aloud, feeling a beam of energy light me up from deep within myself, "that's me."

Part 4

2002–2004

---

*A*s the meth slowly left my body, the reality and gravity of what I was doing began to register. I was leaving, *abandoning*, my wife—and she didn't even know it.

Guilt engulfed me, guilt that had been suppressed, or more like squelched, by the meth. How much longer could I go on not telling her? She had the right to know that I had made irreversible decisions to jettison her from my life and to come out, stay out, and transition to becoming a woman. When at last I thought I had mustered the courage to contact her, I received a call from a woman named Mistress Tara. She lived in North Hollywood. Weeks earlier I had seen her ad for "Bootcamp for Sissymaids" and applied. The offering sounded like it would be similar to a week I had recently spent in New York City living in a house of female domination as a slave, doing the cleaning, running errands, and helping the doms prepare for their clients. Bootcamp for sissymaids was exactly the distraction I needed to postpone a full reckoning of my past, present, and future. No matter that Erin and Joyce had chosen me as their roommate and that I had even begun to settle into my new household. With barely a second thought I took off for Los Angeles for a one-week holiday from my troubles.

I arrived at the Den of Inequity, as the operation was called, fully expecting to be interacting with other slave enrollees. This aspect didn't appeal to me, so it was a pleasant surprise to learn I was to be the sole participant in this bootcamp. Mistress Tara was very kind and friendly during our initial encounter, and, as she explained, this was the one and only time during my stay that she would act as such. Once we got under way with my training, all would change, she said. Mistress Tara even offered me a cold drink, emphasizing that this was the one and only time she would ever do anything for me.

She wasn't kidding. After I finished my drink I was led by leash and collar into the kitchen, fitted with a longer chain, and taken over to a pile of dirty dishes. "Do you know how to wash and dry dishes?" Mistress Tara asked. "Yes, of course," I answered. She sat at the table to observe me. From the moment I started, things were completely wrong. Mistress Tara then showed me how to "assume the position" for my caning; down on all fours, nose to the ground, buttocks raised high so she could get a good smack with her cane. I had to count the switches and thank her for each one. Despite all the hormones and crystal meth residue still coursing through my veins, I felt myself getting hard for the first time in months. As I counted away and thanked her, my erection grew as my bottom began to burn. What was it that made me feel this way? How did my life end up wanting this so badly? Why was I so turned on by this? I had not yet figured out it had a lot to do with the abusive conditions of my childhood. Here already, Mistress Tara was gaining control over my mind, and I was up until 4 a.m. cleaning her kitchen.

Sex and drugs had ruled my life for so long. I wasn't taking meth any longer, but during my recent addiction ordeal, my interest in female domination had escalated to an out-there level. For example, one weekend I took a trip up to Seattle to meet with a dominatrix. She wanted to have me kidnapped and sent away as a purchased slave. She claimed to have buyers, female buyers, and explained how I was to be drugged and shipped in a crate, just like a dog. Once with my new owner and mistress, I was to spend the rest of my life, albeit a short one, as her slave until I was used up and then put down. I actually believed this woman and drove up to Seattle several times to give her money until it finally penetrated my meth haze that I was being played.

The next morning I was taught how to cook one of Mistress Tara's favorite breakfasts: Malt-o-Meal. The image of an ogre eating her porridge didn't occur to me until later, but it fit! Her hot cereal had to be just the right consistency, without lumps in it, and have the correct amount of heated milk and sugar. Anything less would mean assuming the position for punishment, which was liberally applied for the most minor infraction. I had to serve mistress her breakfast in bed, entering her room on my knees, tray extended forward to put over her lap, then bow down to all fours, nose to the ground to await further orders, which often entailed something I might have forgotten, leading to another caning. Mistress Tara truly enjoyed beating me. Though I was never allowed to look up at her, I could feel her energy and voice as she worked to subdue my mind so that I gave myself completely over to her.

She took me to a uniform shop where she selected two classic old-school maid outfits that I wore for the duration of my training. I looked ridiculous in them, and the sales lady laughed when she realized they were for me. Once again I felt myself growing hard. This was unusual not only because for months the HRT had robbed me of erections but because I was able to get into my number without the use of speed to release my inhibitions. I was fitted with several pairs of maid's working shoes, like something out of the 1950s. The full regalia included a corset, panties, garter, and stockings. Our next stop was, of all places, a Home Depot. The superstore offered all sorts of inexpensive items suitable for sessions, Mistress Tara explained, and this was when I learned that

I would be assisting in the prep work for when other mistresses came to the Den of Inequity to see clients. We bought clamps, chain link, duct tape, cleaning supplies—a myriad of stuff. She had a ball going up and down the aisles as we grabbed this and that. When we checked out, I looked around at the other customers, smiling privately, wondering if anyone had any clue as to the real purpose for our cart full of goodies.

The best moments during that intense week were when other mistresses dropped in for scheduled sessions. I got to meet and serve them during down time, in addition to helping them set up for clients. The Den of Inequity had multiple BDSM theme rooms, replete with all the trimmings needed for any kind of scene. One client was into being force-fed. I watched from a private viewing area as the mistress shoved his head into a trough full of mashed up, disgusting-looking food. Others were into milk enemas— which I didn't know was such a popular fetish—and numerous times I found myself running to the market for more cartons. A few got off on suspension bondage, wearing sensory deprivation masks, being beaten, and receiving a "golden shower" (being urinated on). The sessions fascinated me. I was getting an education in the oddness of human sexuality, one that made my stuff seem almost vanilla.

Mistress Tara allowed the mistresses to have playtime with me. I was the obedient slave on whom they could practice bondage, spankings, canings, or whatever. These doms were hot, young, and into it. I got plenty of attention that lit up my loins. My sexual energy came roaring back and a whole new addiction was enveloping me. It was as if I had traded meth for domination. There were also photo shoots for which I was trussed up like a pig and beaten. The photos were for the website to attract business. I was flattered to be chosen for these images, but it was demanding work, and we would stay up until nearly dawn. Afterward, I still had to do my regular chores. Work as a sissymaid never ended inside the Den of Inequity.

It was also thought provoking. In my unique "backstage" role I observed the toil of the job on the mistresses. I saw them struggling with substance abuse issues and pushing themselves to fulfill client fetishes. Who really called the shots? It was the client paying the $300 per hour fee. The client always dictated what turned him on. He got whatever he wanted, no matter that the mistress was supposed to be the one in charge. These doms had to mentally rev up for each session so the client felt completely dominated, yet afterward they complained how ho-hum the whole experience was to them. And when not working they could seem very normal. I learned that many of them had boyfriends they were supporting financially. This more than anything told me the true tale. Though I'd had similar glimmers of insight as a slave in New York, my informed skepticism at that time was short lived. I hadn't been ready to accept the cold unvarnished truth.

I likewise began seeing through Mistress Tara's tough front. What mattered foremost to her was money. I not only paid for my bootcamp but bought food, paid for my uniforms, and covered the Home Depot spree, and other expenses. Moreover, she was hardly the hot mistress portrayed in her photos online, who could've easily been twenty years old. She struggled to fit into her fetish gear and it was not easy to zip her up. She lasted no longer than thirty minutes before needing to change out. Her nightly pint of Häagen-Daz and obligatory two packs of cigarettes didn't help. Yes, she could display cruelty like a true dom, but it mostly came from being a self-centered, narcissistic, greedy, aging woman. One day she checked out my cleaning in the living room and found dust. I was told that I would pay for that, yet then she decided that since I had complained earlier about needing to eat, first she would get me some "food." She took a sheet of newspaper, which she had me tear into pieces, and put them on plate. I was forced to eat the paper without water. Several times I came close to choking and was terrified the paper might get stuck in my throat. The hatred on her face during this punishment suggested true vindictiveness, as if she wanted to seriously hurt me.

The last straw came during an even more life-threatening stunt. I had been in my sleeping cubicle on a short break when my cell phone rang. It was Kristi calling from New Zealand. Hearing her voice in these circumstances disoriented me, and she could tell things weren't right and asked what was going on. As I sought to reassure her that everything was fine, Mistress Tara barged in, snatched my phone and shut it off. Of course, now I would need to be punished. She had me follow her into one of the fantasy rooms where she told me to strip. She then proceeded to tie me up to the ceiling with my arms outstretched and my feet barely touching the floor. Very quickly I felt the blood flow slowing to my wrists. Next, she duct-taped my phone to my hand after first adding a phone number to its speed dial function. I was told I could call that number if my punishment position became too much. A young dom in training named Mistress Amanda was present during all this and I saw a look of deep concern on her face. She knew exactly what I did: my health, quite possibly my life, was at risk. My hands were numb, the sockets of my arms felt ready to pop out, and my feet were likewise becoming numb. This was no mere S/M game. I realized just how psychotic Mistress Tara was, the deep hatred she harbored for anyone who wasn't as miserable as herself. She then announced that she and Mistress Amanda would now be off with my credit card to enjoy a mani/pedi.

This had to be a ruse, no one would do something like this, I thought the second the door slammed shut. As time passed and my hands went completely numb, I became aware with horror that I could no longer move any of my fingers. Even if I had wanted to speed dial for help, I couldn't. I fought with all my heart and soul to keep from panicking, since tugging or pulling myself out of the bondage would only tighten the ropes and further impede blood circulation to my hands. I talked to myself, sang, and appealed to the universe to help me. My arms felt like lead weights and my hands grew swollen, taking on a ghastly white-purplish color. Terror mounted inside me and I started to yell, hoping someone walking outside might hear me. I was sweating profusely and could smell my body odor mingled with the stench of fear. I began to think of my life and my family. This dreamy state intensified as my body went limp and I just dangled there waiting for it all to be over.

The door swung open. There stood Mistress Tara, with a steely cold glare, and Mistress Amanda, whose expression betrayed grave worry. I was let down from my bondage like Christ's dead body from the cross, whereupon I sank meekly to the floor, unable to stand, use my hands, or lift my head. They left the room and I eventually got up and soaked my hands in ice cold water until some feeling came back. This was it. My life had been endangered by a psychopath—there was no way I could remain at the Den of Inequity. Later that night, I quietly packed all my bags, crept down the stairs, got into my car and took off. I stopped at Mel's Diner to enjoy a full breakfast before driving north to my beloved Portland. I sobbed quite a lot, initially with relief at not dying back there, and then with deep sadness. I was lonely, empty; nobody wanted or loved me. I was almost fifty and a failure. At least I knew it was time to finally tell Kristi that our marriage was over, that I would not be coming to New Zealand.

I was so grateful to return to my lesbian household. Erin and Joyce made me feel welcome. Our great conversations about life helped restore my sensibilities, enough that I contacted Kristi's sister. In an email I told her I had come out as a woman, wasn't moving to New Zealand, how it would be best if Kristi and I divorced, and that I didn't want to have any phone discussions with Kristi. I knew she would forward my email. When after several days I hadn't heard from her I thought maybe our breakup was going to be easier than I thought. I was in the process of having a lawyer draw up the divorce papers when one morning Kristi called.

"Don't hang up," she said.

Thus began our grueling final showdown, one full of bitter recriminations and agonizing attack and retreat discussions, all of which did, ultimately, lead us to the conclusion that it was best for us to divorce and go our separate ways—after one last reunion.

The flight to New Zealand was arduous. My passport said I was male yet because I looked more like a woman, there was confusion at customs. I knew this might happen but endured the hassle in order to say goodbye to Kristi and Spunky in person. The visit was highly charged and emotional. I was still feeling withdrawal effects from the crystal meth, which meant I tired out easily and lacked mental clarity and focus. Picking up on my sluggishness, Kristi became very nurturing. She cooked good food, we walked Spunky on the beach every morning, and we even toured the South Island's national parks. New Zealand was gorgeous and had a very agreeable climate and the people were friendly. I could indeed see myself living there. Only there was no way I could go back into the closet to stay with Kristi and Spunky. If I did, I'd be right back to where I started.

On my last morning, we signed the divorce papers before departing for the airport. The way Kristi looked at me I suspected all it would take was for me to say, "Let's try again." I held my tongue. I had considered telling her how the crystal meth addiction had allowed me to come out for good because I had lacked the courage to do so on my own. I thought this might help ease her pain, help her better understand why all this had happened so suddenly. In the end I elected not to, fearing that the truth could backfire and anger her to the point of squelching any hope for a future friendship, something I hoped we could have some day. I said goodbye to Spunky, who cocked his head sideways and watched from the porch as the car backed out of the driveway. Kristi and I didn't say a word en route to the airport. At the terminal for New Zealand Air, I gave her a hug and went inside. I cried for nearly half the flight home. It was one of the worst days of my life. Kristi and Spunky were no longer part of my life, and the future frightened me. I had just enough money to pay for my SRS, which I now planned to schedule after my newest big move. This was the part of the future that had me so scared: I was quitting Portland. I would be moving to New York, where a live-in slave position had opened. Bootcamp for sissymaids might have almost killed me, but the world of submission and female domination still had a grip on me, perhaps all the more so since giving up meth.

*B*y the time I crossed the border into Pennsylvania in my Nissan I had already noticed how many more cars and people there were. This was not the open, empty West, but the urbanized East. I drove into New York City in the middle of the afternoon, rush hour in full swing. The Manhattan skyline awed me from where I sat on the highway, inching toward midtown, where Mistress Anastasia, lived. When I got close enough to park I had my first experience with New York "city blocks." I was eight blocks away from her address, a short walk I assumed. How wrong I was. It took me forever to get to her front door.

Mistress Anastasia turned out to be attractive, polite, and business-like. She gave me a tour of her place, including the complete dungeon in her basement that was well stocked with all the tools of the trade. She was an in-demand dominatrix with a long list of reputable clients who paid her big bucks. Because of her reputation I decided not to get discouraged when I learned that, contrary to what she'd indicated during our phone talks, I couldn't move in right away. I resolved to be patient and work hard to gain her trust and acceptance. I badly wanted this to work out, having driven from Oregon expressly to become a full-time slave. Still, I didn't have much money, and lodging in New York was very expensive. At the end of our interview I asked about cheap places to stay, and she suggested the midtown YMCA. She told me to call in a few days so we could get started with my training, which left me hope in a city that suddenly seemed a whole lot more intimidating without a guaranteed job or place to live.

It grew dark during the trek back to my car and I panicked when I couldn't remember exactly where I'd parked. I spent an hour walking aimlessly up and down those super-sized blocks before locating it—along with a parking ticket for $225 on the windshield. Here it was my first day in New York and I was already feeling the economic pinch of living in one of the most expensive cities in the world. At the YMCA, I got a bunk bed assignment in the girls' dorm and had just laid down, utterly exhausted and longing to relax, when there was a knock on the door. Outside a male staff member stood there asking for me. He told me I couldn't stay and that I would have to come back the next day to see if an individual room was available. I became suspicious that one of the girls had read me and complained to the front desk. But there was nothing I could do. I trudged back to my car with my heavy suitcase and tried to sleep there. It was uncomfortable and people kept walking past all night long. I was a nervous wreck and already missing Portland, sure that I'd made a horrible mistake coming to this city.

I awoke the next morning to a traffic cop staring at me though the passenger-side window. It was 7:15 a.m., and the cop informed me I had one minute to move my car or get (another) parking ticket as well as get towed. I started up my car, still half-asleep, dazed, hungry, thirsty, and desperately needing a bathroom. Back over at the YMCA, I was met with a hostile reception. No single room was available and I was offered a bunk with a male. This infuriated me, but I had no alternative. I fetched my suitcase from my car—I triple checked that it was parked legally—and lugged it into the hotel. I asked at the front desk where the elevator was. There was none. There was also no air-conditioning. I finally reached the top floor of the building, found my room, and went in. My new roommate turned over in his bed, his smelly, toenail fungus feet sticking out, looked at me, and asked groggily, "Are you a man or a woman?" How tactful. "Guess," I replied in my most feminine voice. After a shower and some annoying small talk, I dozed off, dreaming of my green Oregon, its forest waterfalls, pristine coastal beaches, nice people, and mellow Portland—a city friendly to queers—unlike this hellhole I had impulsively let myself fall into.

Welcome to New York.

The YMCA had a maximum length of stay of ten days. I began to answer roommate ads and was shocked by the prices of even a small room in a lousy apartment building. Luckily, I got a lead on a place up near the George Washington Bridge that seemed like a good fit, with two women, Megan and Rachel. After a positive telephone chat they invited me over. I showed up and we hit it off, helped out by a joint I rolled full of Oregon pot. We passed it around and after ten minutes they both stopped talking and just sat there staring straight ahead. I asked if everything was okay. They looked at me, giggling, and said they'd never in their lives been so stoned. The next day they called and offered me the room. It cost $750 per month, with the standard additional $750 for last month's rent, plus a $350 security deposit, for a tiny bedroom squeezed between their larger rooms.

New York turned out to be a blessing in one regard: the access to free social services. At the famous Callen-Lorde Community

Health Care Center, in the West Village, medical professionals helped me monitor my HRT. A lesbian physician whom I developed a crush on took a keen interest in making sure I was physically ready for my upcoming surgery, which I had decided to have done in Thailand. I also received counseling there by a grad student who helped me identify and get through the remaining fallout over my breakup with Kristi, whom I missed. I even got free dental work to fix my teeth; they were in desperate need of attention after the havoc wreaked by crystal meth, which activates acids in the mouth that eat away tooth enamel. I bought a gym membership at the McBurney YMCA, where I swam laps. At this Y, the staff did not question my gender. And since the women's locker room had semiprivate changing stalls, I was able to come and go without worry. The gym was near Mistress Anastasia's and I got into the habit of stopping by her place after my swim. I was still determined to make things work with her and looked forward to that big day when she'd say, "Move in, slave!"

Only it never happened. In fact, early on she said to drop the mistress thing and just call her Anastasia. We became more like friends. I'd drop by, smoke pot with her, and we'd have long philosophical discussions. She was very interested in my upcoming SRS, which we talked about extensively. Other times her temper would flare and she'd revert to being a dom, ordering me to clean her place and the dungeon. Though our relationship was strange, she, like me, had midwestern roots, and I felt connected to her, not to mention attracted. She promised me a pagan ceremony after my SRS, a pledge she later fulfilled in her dungeon. I still recall the room lit up with candles and the shadows cast by the flames dancing across the brick walls. Anastasia helped me down the steep stairs, for I was still in pain from the surgery. Then, one by one, six mistresses came down to see me and my new vagina, shown off by a skimpy pair of panties. Everyone was sincerely amazed at how natural my vagina looked. Finally, Anastasia arrived and performed a Wicca blessing. That special occasion was the last time we saw each other.

$\mathcal{T}$he anonymity of New York is fantastic. The second you walk out the front door you're surrounded by millions, not knowing a single soul. And yet one day while crossing a busy Manhattan avenue I practically knocked into Mistress Amanda, whom I had last seen that awful final night at the Den of Inequity. We both were so surprised to bump into each other that we started gabbing right in the middle of the intersection until honking car horns got us moving along. She wanted me to meet her new full-time slave, who had a high income and had set her up in a midtown high rise where he paid all the bills. I really wasn't that interested in meeting this guy, but since I liked Mistress Amanda I called her two days later and agreed to swing by. I arrived at a deluxe building with a doorman, who phoned up to announce me.

Amanda's spacious apartment had a stunning view of the Hudson River and New Jersey. She had prepared some snacks and drinks, and she invited me to sit. We relaxed and got caught up. I learned she had quit the Den of Inequity shortly after my boot-camp ordeal; she completely agreed that Mistress Tara was insane. During our gossip session, the phone rang. Her slave had returned home from work—he lived in another condo in the same building—and he was begging to be allowed over.

"Absolutely," Mistress Amanda said and then mentioned there was a special guest here for him to meet. "Mistress Denise wants to put you through your paces."

Mistress Denise? I was flabbergasted.

Mistress Amanda would hear none of my protests, explaining, "Mistress Denise, didn't you know that the best doms come from being the best bottoms?" She added, "I happen to know you were one of the best bottoms I ever met in LA, so you must go with the flow on this one and see how you feel. Empower yourself, Mistress Denise. Your time is upon you."

With a speech like that, how could I refuse? Now we had to prepare for the slave's session. This was the easy part, all routine for me as I helped get the equipment ready: leather hood, restraints, leg spreader, ball gag for after he was done being allowed to speak, doggie bowl, leather collar and leash, paddles, two long canes—all the usual stuff, along with a large dog kennel we dragged out of the closet. Mistress Amanda dug out a pair of long black leather boots that fit me perfectly and went well with my short skirt and cute top. In the mirror, I really did look the part of a dominatrix. And with my regular makeup and a recent blowout, I looked pretty hot for a forty-nine-year-old.

Mistress Denise, I said to myself. It has a ring to it. Maybe it will grow on me, who knows?

There was a soft knock at the door and the slave was admitted. Despite being on time he was chided for being late and forced to crawl into the living room, eyes down, and halt in front of where I was seated comfortably on the couch. He was a black man around my age and still dressed in his office attire. She made him kiss my boots and told him to introduce himself. That's when he said, "I'm just a no good, stupid nigger slave who deserves to be punished, just a no good nigger slave is all I am." I had directly observed or heard of many wild and freaky numbers, but this was a new, unsettling one. I didn't say a word, letting Mistress Amanda run the session during which I occasionally stroked him with a whip. I was doing the things to him that I would've wanted done to me, and the reversal made me see the connection of how a good bottom can make a good top, or in my case, dominatrix. "Mistress Denise" suddenly made sense.

After dismissing the slave, Mistress Amanda put $75 in my hand. I protested, but she insisted, saying he would want me back again and told me she had other clients who would want me too.

"Are you interested?"

"Absolutely," I answered.

I left in a daze and headed for the subway station thinking about everything that had just happened. I didn't get any sexual thrill out of being a dom, it was just an easy $75. I had considered this just-a-job angle before, but now with firsthand experience the veil was really lifted on the dominatrix world. It was all a gimmick built around the erotic fantasies of the human sexual experience. The façade had crumbled. I went from Slave Denise to Mistress Denise. I was in it for the money, honey, and would never look back.

Days prior to my departure for Bangkok my weed supply dwindled to practically nothing. I asked my roommates where I could get some and learned all I needed to do was call a phone number and it would be delivered to the front door. A pot *delivery* service? I was incredulous. Still skeptical, the next day I called the number they gave me. It was a pager, so I entered my number. Someone named James called me back in ten minutes. I told him that Megan was my roommate and that I needed a delivery. He said he'd call me back from outside the building in about an hour. I hung up the phone still not believing it was this easy to score weed in New York.

James, true to his word, called back. But he didn't come up to our apartment; instead I had to go down to his car and do the deal there. It would have been far better, I thought, if the transaction were to happen inside the apartment, which would have provided more comfort for all in a private, relaxed atmosphere. I selected my weed out of a briefcase but could not open the bags to inspect the contents for fragrance because they were sealed shut. I kept thinking how differently I would run a service like this. Still, it was a great model and I was envious of James's little pot business and how much easy money he must bring in; I was in his car for five minutes and his pager went off three times. I asked him how he managed to obtain so many customers. He proudly me told that he'd bought the business from a friend for $50,000 several years ago and was doing really well. I asked if he needed an assistant, since I wasn't working except for an occasional dominatrix session, but he said he already had one. I walked away from the car with my mind in a swirl. His pot was nowhere near as good as what I had brought from the West Coast, and it was three times the price.

Woman or no woman, after I returned from Bangkok I was plunged right back into poverty. Job hunting was complicated by the fact that I wasn't completely healed. I had to dilate three times per day for forty-five minutes a shot. Sticking to this regimen was imperative so I didn't "close up" and thereby throw away the results of my surgery. My fiftieth birthday rolled around the last week of December. Being a half-century old was a sobering milestone, to say the least. I rallied, telling myself, you've lived almost fifty years in your other life, so now you're going to live the next fifty years in your new life! To celebrate I made a batch of pot brownies and with friends in tow went to see the final installment of the *Lord of the Rings* trilogy. It was a perfect escape from my worries over money and finding a job.

Pink Floyd once sang, "Desperation is the English way." That's how I felt the afternoon I called my mother to ask for money. With rent almost due, it was either appeal to her or move into my car. Never in my wildest imagination did I think it would come down to this, depending on my mother at this point in life to survive. Were she to say yes, I'd already sworn to myself she would be the vey first person on my growing list of debtors to pay back as soon as I could. Mom asked me how much and I told her $2,500. I knew this amount wouldn't last long, but I couldn't bear to ask for more. After a long pause on the other end that sent me into a panic, she asked for my bank information. Two days later the money arrived.

My big hope was to secure a job at the New York Philharmonic, not so far-fetched given my past success at the Oregon Symphony. After persistence I got an appointment to see the assistant marketing director. The day of my interview she seemed prepared for me, for on her desk I noticed all my mailed materials. Quickly, however, I got the impression that she didn't really care about the pitch I'd carefully prepared. She did not need someone like me coming in to propose a fund-raising idea that would add to her workload and even potentially threaten her position. I realized I should've been talking with someone more senior, but it was too late. In a desperate bid, I started name-dropping executives in the symphony business I had worked for, one of them being, I knew from my research, a person she had worked with at the Aspen Music Festival. This seemed to bring her around, so, feeling I had nothing to lose, I outed myself, hoping to rouse some compassion in her. This cold fish just stared at me—through me, beyond me—and the interview was over. I exited the building barely able to hold back tears of disappointment and despair as the sidewalk greeted me with the freezing dusk. Had I been discriminated against for being trans? It seemed so.

With my mother's loan running out, I came up with a rather unorthodox scheme to find employment. At a copy shop I had my résumé blown up large enough to fill a piece of foam board. Doing the same on another piece, I wired the two together to create a sandwich board. Looking like Wimpy the Hamburger Man from the Popeye cartoon, I headed off to the mecca of capitalism: Trump Tower. How could I go wrong handing out my résumé in front of that building where so many extremely wealthy people entered and exited? I fantasized that I might meet the Donald himself, who at that time in New York was admired for his brash, populist style. My guerilla-style job search won me some encouraging smiles and not a few hostile stares. Finally, a uniformed guy from Trump security stepped over to ask what I was doing. I told him and he left, though very soon another security guy in a blazer approached. He said that because I was not moving, I was loitering.

"No problem," I said. "I'll walk back and forth." He shook his head in a damning way but left me alone. I knew Trump security was watching from somewhere up in that tower. Sure enough, yet another security agent appeared. This one, in an expensive suit, starched white shirt, black tie, earpiece, and dark sunglasses, looked straight out of that year's hit film *The Matrix.* "Good morning, Agent Smith," I ventured, using humor to establish rapport. Agent Smith failed to get the joke. He dryly read me the riot act, saying they didn't want to call the police and have me arrested but would if I didn't leave immediately. It was illegal to hand out flyers on a New York City public sidewalk without a permit, he told me. Trump's security had confirmed this with the Trump organization's attorney office. Secretly, I felt proud that I'd managed to make it onto the radar screen of a powerful law firm somewhere, interrupting those highly paid individuals' day to deal with little old me. I prepared to leave but not before asking Agent Smith if he wanted a résumé. "Will you please give it to the Donald"? I asked. He took one.

I didn't abandon my tactic, I just relocated. I spent several days around town handing out my résumé in the snow and cold. Full of confidence, I then took a few days off to handle the many phone calls and emails that I was sure were to come. I wanted to be in a comfortable setting for the onslaught of employer inquiries. Not a single phone call, not a single email. This shocked me beyond belief. I was really at a loss at how to find a job in this tough town.

The morning after my fruitless phone and email vigil, I awoke early to move my car to conform to the three-day rule governing parked vehicles. My spot was less than a block away, but when I got to where my car was supposed to be, it wasn't there. Confused, I rewalked the route, thinking I'd made an error, but I ended up back exactly where my car should've been. A lady sitting in her car, getting ready to move, asked me if I was looking for my car. I nodded. "Do you drive a dark green Nissan with Oregon license plates?" she asked. I numbly shook my head again. "Well, they came by ten minutes ago and towed it." She speculated that it was taken by the city parking enforcement agency, which confiscates vehicles with overdue parking tickets. If I didn't claim it within seven days, she told me, my car would be auctioned.

I wanted to collapse right there and cry, only I was too angry. I saw this exactly for what it was: a scam, a predation perpetuated by the city on unknowing owners of vehicles who owe money that lets it "legally" profit many times over what was originally owed. I raced back to my apartment and contacted the city to find out how to get my car back. The city wanted $1,200 to release my car; money I didn't have. But I knew that if I lost it for good, I'd be stranded, robbed of the only backup place I had to sleep. I was suddenly looking at becoming homeless. With no alternative, I contacted Kristi in New Zealand. I'd done her a huge favor a year earlier by helping her get her employment card, collecting the documents she needed. She was very friendly on the phone, and said she would immediately wire me the money. I felt incredibly grateful and mentally added her name below my mother's on the list of those to one day pay back in full. The difficult part of the call was hearing about her new boyfriend and how happy she was. I became angry, wondering how much in fact she had actually loved me. But I stopped myself and accepted her good fortune, knowing we would both move on quicker the happier we both were.

The day the money came I was right against the deadline and rushed to the address where my car was supposed to be. Only it wasn't there. The bastards had already towed it to another location, where the auction was to be held the very next day. "It's a nice, small car," I recalled the neighborhood lady saying. "It'll sell in a second." I still had a few hours to get over to the Bronx, pay my bill, and retrieve my car. In ninety minutes I was at the "collection site": a fortified, bulletproof trailer with a line of people ten deep, each person waiting to be called in turn to the tiny pay window, where only cash was accepted. I was beside myself with disgust. I knew money was being doled out all over the place on this car scam the city had going. I finally got to the window, which was covered by a five-inch-thick piece of glass to protect those behind it. And what about all of us standing there with large amounts of cash? Where was our protection? I was fuming as I counted out twelve hundred-dollar bills and slapped them down in the metal tray. After my money was examined and recounted, I was given an official-looking piece of paper. That was it—no instructions on what to do next. When I asked, I found out that my car wasn't there but at the "confiscation lot," which closed in twenty minutes. I'd have new fines if I didn't get there immediately. I was lucky to find a cab in that area of the Bronx and reached the lot with six minutes to spare. Like the other place, there was a small office with a secure pay drawer. The guy looked at my piece of paper, stamped it, and demanded $75. "For what?" I angrily inquired. "Additional paperwork," he replied with a sneer. Another scam, but I handed over the money. The clerk let me inside the compound and took me to my car. This whole shakedown so unnerved me that for the first time since arriving to New York, I began to actively plan my exit and return to Oregon. If I was going to be homeless, I stood a better chance of coping with it there than here.

I left New York in late March 2004, after less than a year. I had made new friends, whose fortitude I admired. Megan wrote me a check for $350, telling me I'd need gas money to make it to Oregon. Another name added to my creditors' list. Though I had struggled in New York, happiness never eluded me. I was a complete woman now, so different from when I'd arrived the previous August. Nothing could ever change that, and the greatest lesson I learned there was to never give up, always keep fighting and believe in yourself, because eventually you will persevere. As I drove back through Pennsylvania my head was full of thoughts about the future. All that receded from my mind the nearer I got to Wisconsin and the impending visit I had planned with my mother. I had phoned ahead to ask if I could see her. She had not sounded thrilled by the idea, yet she agreed.

Much like the phone call from the Anchorage airport en route to Bangkok that had ended with my mother begging me not to follow through with sex reassignment surgery and "hurt myself," this visit was in no way healing. As I stood at her front door and tried to hug her, she backed away like I had the bubonic plague. She had trouble even looking at me when we sat at the kitchen table and I attempted to have a conversation. She made me feel terrible, like I'd done something horribly wrong. It was as if she would've preferred I'd been a bank robber, an ex-con, even a child molester, anything but the trans woman who was now her daughter. Finally finding her voice, she poured out a litany of accusatory questions. "Why?" she asked. How could I do this to her? How could I do this to our family? Where did she go wrong with me? I tried to explain that it was no one's fault, I was born this way, and that it had been my big secret kept from her, the family, and everyone else all my life. Then I turned the tables, reminding her of events that had revealed what I was about.

I asked about the Greendale police talking to her at the station after the stolen golf clubs incident. . . . About the panties found on the basement stairs and the talk she had with dad about it. . . . About the time she lifted the blanket in my bedroom when I was pretending to sleep, so she could see what I was wearing.

To every question her answer was the same: "I don't remember that!"

I knew she did remember, only she was in complete denial. The signs were there in my childhood and adolescence, but she chose each time to turn a blind eye, to not deal with it, to turn away from me and make me feel like I was something inhuman, some weirdo who was destined to fail in life. I knew my father had been the same way, and despite forgiving him on his deathbed, I still believed he was as culpable and guilty as she was. How ironic that my parents, by their inaction and refusal to come to terms with who I was, made me feel guilty and ashamed about myself. Did they not realize that they were scarring me for life? Setting me up for a life of drug and alcohol abuse that nearly killed me?

And here my mother was doing it again, making me feel terrible for coming out as Denise so that I might at last find happiness and live my life for me, not for someone else. That was the moment it really hit me hard. My mother was more concerned about what others would think than about the happiness and well being of her adult child. I couldn't help but recall my brother-in law, Steve, the one who had discovered my secret the time he opened my car trunk to fix my speakers and found my girl clothes. He had committed suicide a couple of years earlier. This tense exchange with my mom made me feel sure she would have preferred a similar outcome for me. That she could've buried Dennis, thereby never, ever having to deal with Denise.

But it wasn't going to work out that way. I didn't commit suicide, overdose, or drink myself to death. I was a survivor, and here I was in all my glory as a new woman, a woman of confidence, happiness, and certainty. Nothing was going to stop me from here on out. I'd come way too far to let things shut me down now. I had a new destiny waiting for me in Oregon. I would prevail; I could sense it.

Standing up to leave, I thanked her for the loans that had saved me in New York and told her one day, that money would be repaid in full. But she wouldn't look at me, and I had to contain my boiling anger. I thought of all the work I'd done to look nice for her on this first visit as Denise. I had stopped to have my nails done and my hair styled, and I had made an effort to dress sharply. All for naught. I urged her to get up and walk me to the front door, but she wouldn't budge. When I tried to hug her, she cringed away from me. This rejection cut into me like a dagger. Recovering as best I could, I walked to the door, turning once to see her face buried in her hands. I drove away feeling a deep, wounding pity for her and the unhappiness she was inflicting on herself by refusing to embrace the wonderful change in me, who had blossomed into this new being and was now ready to strive for the happiness and focus that had eluded me for so long.

On my first day back in Portland I bent down to kiss the ground. How wonderful to return to friendly stoner Portland, where the weed was great and the price was right. I had a roof over my head: Erin and Joyce were letting me stay with them until I found something permanent. I was highly motivated to find a job, any job, to pay bills while my new grand plan came together: I was going to launch a modest, New York–inspired pot delivery service providing small amounts of good weed, thanks to a friend I had in Humboldt County. My chief goal was to land a real job, either in the arts or travel industry.

In the midst of job hunting, I took a weekend off to venture down to Humboldt and test the waters. I had only enough cash to buy two ounces of a high-quality weed called Train Wreck. My plan was to break that into grams and several eighths of an ounce. I instinctively knew that professional packaging was key, so I bought three-inch square bags to make the small amounts look attractive. Factoring in gas money for the thousand-mile round trip and other expenses, I wasn't able to afford even a cheap motel, so I slept in my car at a state day park, ignoring the signs expressly forbidding camping. I even changed into pajamas before putting my seat back and covering myself with a blanket. Soon after dozing off, I was woken by a bright light shinning in my face. Blinking to open my eyes, I saw a cop glaring at me, motioning for me to roll down the window. He gruffly asked what I was doing here. My first inclination was to mouth off. "What the hell do you think I'm doing here? Sleeping, until your sorry ass woke me up, and in the middle of a great dream too." But I had weed in the car and quickly adopted a conciliatory attitude. "Well, officer, I'm a diabetic and I was having a hypoglycemic episode and had to pull over to rest, otherwise I would've passed out at the wheel and caused a serious accident." His suspicion melted into sympathy. After running a license check he returned to the car and asked how much longer I needed to be here.

"Till dawn."

"Dawn!"

"Yeah, this was a serious attack and I need to rest."

"Well, just move on as soon as you can," he stammered and then left.

The park was on a stretch of gorgeous rugged coast and soon after dawn I was up and down on the beach where I smoked some of my purchase. *Wow.* Train Wreck was the real deal. I made it back to Portland and broke up the ounces. My total take would be modest—so long as I resisted smoking up my product. I had no market yet and that, I knew, could take time to develop. It also was the riskiest part of the effort: actually letting people know that I had smoke for sale. And not the usual Oregon green crap, but bona fide Humboldt County Train Wreck, the best stuff around. Early on I resolved to build my business on certain principles: quality, fair pricing, reliability, punctuality, and privacy. If I adhered to these principles, I was sure I'd eventually be successful, at least profitable enough to pay my bills and reduce my debt.

Meanwhile, to make ends meet, I took random jobs. Hired on by the Democratic National Committee to do door-to-door fund-raising, I endured exhausting long hours at minimum wage only to be fired when I didn't raise enough money. The attitude of the local DNC office infuriated me. "So you're supposed to stand for the common man, for women, for the poor, for minorities?" I shouted at the manager. "Look at you, acting just like Republicans, you bunch of weasel hypocrites!" A better-paying gig came along working as a perfume rep for Elizabeth Arden brands. At Meier & Frank, a department store in downtown Portland that later became a Macy's, I sold bottles of Elizabeth Taylor's White Diamonds and Britney Spears's Curious. I had a lot of experience in sales and ended up one of the top saleswomen on the floor. My success brought envy. A coworker read me somehow and one day she used the wrong pronoun when speaking to me in front of a sales rep. Though seething inside, I just smiled. What she couldn't even begin to understand was how much this high-fem job validated me as a complete woman, boosting my self-esteem and making me just so happy. The part-time job had the potential to go full time, but fortunately that didn't happen. Had it, I might have given up my home delivery business.

Ever since the day I rode in my friend's car in Milwaukee and experienced my very first amazing pot high, marijuana had been a mainstay for me. I'd ingested tons of other substances and suffered from crippling addictions to both crystal meth and alcohol. Pot, however, was always too life enhancing to dream of giving up for good. It was the thing that had created community for me in numerous situations and saved me from isolation and withdrawal. The idea of community, of a tribe, was deeply embedded in my idea of becoming Portland's go-to pot delivery lady. So with my great product in hand, I set about selling it. Or trying to. Though I was quite willing to go out and promote myself, whether at parties or to total strangers, sales were just about dead. It was hard to get a pulse going. What encouraged me to keep at it was the response to the few home deliveries that I scraped together: people loved my weed, and they loved the professionalism that I brought to the job. Eventually that caught on, referrals trickled in, and my business began to grow. The often repeated story about me by customers was how I was the best pot connection they'd ever had and the delivery aspect was the frosting on the cake.

Just as I had innovated in previous jobs, I came up with unique marketing tools for this one. An early popular one was Grab-a-Gram. I put wrapped grams into a paper bag, each labeled with its particular strain. The customer shook the bag and reached in for a surprise gram. I also started selling Humboldt "shake." Shake is the small bits of plant that break off from the meaty buds. The growers gave it to me for free, underestimating its potency. "Denise, you mean to say you want that trash?" they said. "Take all you want."

I did take it and called the sales from it my "trash to cash" program, likening my discovery of this profitable byproduct to the California gold rush, only my slogan was: there's green in them thar hills. In fact, Humboldt led the nation in pot production and was making a lot of folks rich.

It was still early in my new business and I continued to look for a career job. I was a finalist for a key position with Portland Center Stage, a local arts heavyweight. During a lunch with the development director, I sensed that although he wanted to hire me, he was afraid to do so because I was trans; my difference might be a handicap for an organization with heavy corporate sponsorship. It was bitterly disappointing to see this type of discrimination play out in Portland, which I believed was generally a very open-minded town.

While working as a barista at Lewis and Clark College, I became popular with many of the students and faculty. I crossed the line, however, when I introduced Grab-a-Gram to the grad students. Sales boomed, but someone ratted on me and I was fired. I managed to stave off financial hardship by a gradual uptick in pot sales. Then came April 20 that year. Suddenly, I was struggling to keep up with deliveries. I mentioned this to a favorite customer, an art student at Portland State University. She laughed, saying, "It must be due to 420 coming up."

"You mean Hitler's birthday?" I responded naively, me, ever the student of history.

She laughed even harder, explaining to me about 420, or universal "Pot Day," which was celebrated around the world and was huge in Portland. April 20 apparently became synonymous with weed owing to a group of stoners at a California high school who regularly met after class at 4:20. Thanks to them, I set a new record on the big day. My ambition and idealism had paid off; my little business had made it.

I finally did well enough that I was able to pay back those people to whom I owed money. The very first person I paid back was my mother. I sent her two lump payments with a thank you card. I felt very good about righting my financial ship. I had integrity once again and felt balanced and complete as a new woman who was no longer "in arrears" or dependent on anyone. In the one-on-one service I was providing, a lot of customers inevitably opened up to me about their lives, goals, and dreams. Many customers became friends. Some of these friends invited me into their lives and even, from time to time, their work. Indeed, the reason I ended up in *The Auteur* and in 2008 found myself at the Tribeca Film Festival was because the film's writer and director and its producer were guys I met through my little delivery service.

Thinking about that whole movie experience now I see how it had its earliest beginnings in those swirling green waters of the Wisconsin lake at my grandparents' cottage. That day when I almost drowned but didn't because a calming energy appeared, a spirit that throughout my life has intervened to rescue me from certain harm, sometimes manifesting as that little voice telling me

I was making a mistake, cautioning me about denying my true self. I heard that voice as I was walking down the proverbial aisle on my wedding day and ignored it. I heard that voice in Thailand when my wife Kristi and I visited the famous Emerald Buddha. You are a woman, the voice told me. It's a voice I often ignored or tuned out with drugs and alcohol. And so when I reflect again on that visit to see my mother shortly after becoming Denise, I try to treat her "I don't remember" responses with the same empathy I've extended to myself for my own past denials.

As a result of personal pain caused by my own actions and treatment by my family, community, and institutions like the Catholic Church, I've gone from darkness into light many times. Still, I see it all now as part of the same journey, the one that brought me to Denise.

Epilogue

$\mathcal{A}$m I happy as a woman? There is no simple answer to this question. I gave up so much to become Denise. I walked away from the love of my life, whom I still care about to this day. That was the hardest part. I spent a lifetime drinking, smoking, and doing drugs, because it allowed me to run away from who I authentically was. I spent decades in the closet, didn't believe in myself, learned to lie consummately, and struggled to avoid turning my frustration at who I was into violence against myself and others—a battle I nearly lost. I'd probably still be Dennis if it weren't for one thing: the crystal meth. I could have remained Dennis and lived out my life, maybe not the happiest person, but functional. There were many times when "Denise" was the furthest thing from my mind, especially when I was with Kristi. It was the meth that allowed Denise out of the box, further out than she had ever been. And then one day she would not go back in, even after I had quit taking that nasty, destructive drug. Before I found the wherewithal to stop I very nearly squandered the money I had saved for my sex reassignment surgery, which lately is being called gender confirmation surgery (and in the old days it was simply "a sex change"). My meth addiction helped bring out Denise to a degree that made her unstoppable but it also very nearly robbed me of the chance to get the surgery I had always longed for. Money—which I have always worked hard for—allowed for me to board a flight and fly halfway around the world to get a made-in-Bangkok vagina, and money generally has made things easier for me all around. I have been able to enjoy my life as Denise at a higher level and have gradually become more comfortable in my womanhood.

That lengthy qualification out of the way, yes, I am happy as Denise. I think about my decision to transition every single day. Each morning I wake up here in my little piece of paradise on Kauai and express my gratitude that I was able to do this. Recently I read about a transgender girl in Seattle who is transitioning at the age of seventeen. There is so much more awareness out there on gender dysphoria than when I was her age. I have shared my own story in these pages—truly, there is so much more to tell; the unedited version of what you have read was quadruple in length—to add my voice to the growing choir of trans voices, providing increased visibility and paths to greater understanding and respect. My decisions have been a mixed bag, I'm the first to admit. Yet when I am dealt a bad day or find myself contemplating the *what if*'s of my future, I am so glad that the biggest *what if* no longer plagues me or breaks my stride. I'm Denise. That in and of itself makes me feel like fortune's favorite daughter.

LIVING OUT

Gay and Lesbian Autobiographies

Two Novels: "Development" and "Two Selves"
Bryher

The Hurry-Up Song: A Memoir of Losing My Brother
Clifford Chase

In My Father's Arms: A Son's Story of Sexual Abuse
Walter A. de Milly III

*Lawfully Wedded Husband: How My Gay Marriage Will Save
the American Family*
Joel Derfner

Midlife Queer: Autobiography of a Decade, 1971–1981
Martin Duberman

Self-Made Woman
Denise Chanterelle DuBois

The Black Penguin
Andrew Evans

*The Man Who Would Marry Susan Sontag: And Other Intimate
Literary Portraits of the Bohemian Era*
Edward Field

Body, Remember: A Memoir
Kenny Fries

In the Province of the Gods
Kenny Fries

Travels in a Gay Nation: Portraits of LGBTQ Americans
Philip Gambone

Secret Places: My Life in New York and New Guinea
Tobias Schneebaum

Wild Man
Tobias Schneebaum

Sex Talks to Girls: A Memoir
Maureen Seaton

Treehab: Tales from My Natural, Wild Life
Bob Smith

Outbound: Finding a Man, Sailing an Ocean
William Storandt